WHITETAIL WINTER

WHITETAIL WINTER

SEASONS OF THE WHITETAIL
BOOK TWO

Text by John J. Ozoga

WILLOW CREEK PRESS

Minocqua, Wisconsin

PHOTOGRAPHY:

Charles J. Alsheimer, pp. 2, 10, 37, 53, 77, 82, 97, 113, 119, 122, 124, 125, 127, 132, 133, 148.

Donald M. Jones, pp. 5, 29, 31, 50, 91, 114, 118, 141, 147.

Jeff Richter, pp. 8, 32, 47, 55, 87, 94, 108, 134, 125.

Denver Bryan, pp. 12, 36, 54, 64, 72, 106.

Leonard Lee Rue, III, pp. 14, 17, 74, 98, 100, 144.

Lance Krueger, pp. 16, 30, 49, 128, 140.

Bill Kinney, pp. 18, 40, 65, 68, 73.

Judd Cooney, pp. 19, 44, 66, 67, 92, 120, 136.

Greg Gersbach, pp. 20, 43, 121.

Bill Marchel, pp. 22, 26, 33, 41, 58, 79, 80, 86, 89, 95, 107, 112, 115, 139, 146, 151, 155, 156, 157.

Jeanne Drake, pp. 24, 27.

Bill Lea, pp. 25, 28, 38, 48, 60, 63, 85, 96, 103, 111, 130, 131, 137.

Tim Christie, pp. 34, 57, 109.

Len Rue, Jr., pp. 39, 129.

Richard P. Smith, pp. 45, 62, 81, 126, 142, 143, 145, 150, 152, 153.

Michael H. Francis, pp. 52, 71, 105, 117.

Al Cornell, p. 56.

Jeff Bunker, p. 61.

Mike Biggs, p. 160.

Designed by Patricia Bickner Linder

Published by WILLOW CREEK PRESS, P.O. Box 147, Minocqua, WI 54548

For information on other Willow Creek titles, write or call 1-800-850-WILD.

ISBN 1-57223-027-4

Printed in Canada.

Library of Congress Cataloging-in-Publication Data

Ozoga, John J.
    Whitetail winter / text by John J. Ozoga.
        p.   cm. — (Seasons of the whitetail ; bk. 2)
    ISBN 1-57223-027-4 (alk. paper)
    1. White-tailed deer. 2. Winter. I. Title. II. Series: Ozoga, John J. Seasons of the whitetail ; bk. 2.
    QL737.U55095 1995
    599.73'57—dc20   95-10901
                                 CIP

ACKNOWLEDGEMENTS

Research I conducted in the Cusino Wildlife Research Station's square-mile enclosure was unique, primarily because locally severe winters and many talented assistants made it possible to annually live-trap and examine each white-tailed deer in our study herd. Such a routine allowed me to manipulate herd size and composition by carefully selecting animals for reintroduction, a precision not possible in studies of free-ranging deer.

Cusino's annual census had to be completed in March, during a fairly brief period when fetuses carried by pregnant does were large enough to show on radiograms but before snow melt rendered deer trapping untenable. Needless to say, not all deer were cooperative, and things did occasionally go haywire. Capturing the last animal each year was always a monumental task creating many anxious moments.

Several hundred people, including many Michigan Department of Natural Resources employees, Michigan Corrections people (including some enthusiastic residents), university cooperators, private citizens, and family members, helped me during 30 trap-outs. My sincere thanks to all of those involved. As long as I live, my thoughts will stray every March to the challenges of the annual Cusino enclosure deer trap-out and to those that shared in the struggle. Most of all, thanks, Jan, for your support and the many sacrifices you made each March.

Although I've worked with many members of the news media, I'd especially like to acknowledge the cooperation of Buck LeVasseur of TV-6, Marquette, Michigan, and Bob Gwizdz of the Booth News Services, Lansing, Michigan. I'm deeply indebted to both for their frequent coverage of my research efforts and for the wonderful job they did in promoting *Whitetail Autumn*.

If it were not for the work conducted by dedicated researchers like Orrin Rongstad, who has written the foreword to this book and kindly reviewed the text, and many others like him, the ways of wintering whitetails would still be largely a mystery. Thanks, Orrin, and to all the rest of you, for advancing our knowledge of the elusive whitetail and for contributing information that helped make this book possible.

I'd like to extend a special thank you to Chuck and Tom Petrie for their editing, photo selecting, and myriad tasks involved in putting together a book such as this. Above all, Chuck and Tom, thanks for the opportunity and for your vote of confidence.

Also, my sincere thanks and compliments to all those that contributed their superb photographs that vividly illustrate the events illustrating the whitetail's winter — indeed, you people are masters of your trade.

DEDICATION

To Mom and Dad. Thanks for instilling within me,
long ago, the drive to accomplish things such as this.

CONTENTS

FOREWORD

I was extremely pleased when John Ozoga told me that he was going to shift his major efforts from research on the white-tailed deer and writing technical papers, to writing books and popular articles. There has been more research and more scientific articles written on white-tailed deer than practically any other species. However, scientific articles are not light, easy reading that most people enjoy.

John Ozoga has been a very productive deer researcher and has published many important papers contributing to our knowledge of this complex species. He now has demonstrated that he can also put his vast personal knowledge, and synthesize the vast scientific literature, into a form that is easily read and understood by the general public.

The four books in John's "Seasons of the Whitetail" will be something that everyone interested in white-tailed deer will

The duration and severity of winter weather, more than any other factor, determines which whitetail individuals will live to pass on their genetic material to future generations.

benefit from reading and owning. I don't know of any biologist in this country that is more qualified to write this series. John's research, conducted over a period of 30 years, has included studies on deer movements, reproduction, behavior, nutrition, and almost every other aspect of deer biology. Because John did most of his research in northern Michigan, where winters are often severe, he is especially qualified to write *Whitetail Winter.*

My research on the white-tailed deer started during the winter of 1964-65, a winter in which the snow depth in the area where I worked in central Minnesota was 42 inches on the first of April. My 30 years of deer research using radio transmitters to determine movements and mortality factors have made me appreciate the importance of the interactions of weather, habitat, hunting, and social organization on the whitetail's distribution and abundance.

The whitetail's winter is the most variable and complex of the four seasons. Winter is the time of year when most long movements occur in deer populations. Reasons why deer move seasonally or how their specific movements got started is not fully known. If most deer in an area have seasonal movements, it is obvious that those that move survive better than those that don't move. Whether the cause is lack of food and starvation, predators, or hunting by man is not clear. The cause may not have to manifest itself every year; once a family group learns a trait, it may last for years. In the snowbelt, I believe that snow depth is the most critical factor. An infrequent severe winter may be enough to perpetuate the trait. In other areas where seasonal movements also occur, hunting appears to be the cause.

Winter is generally considered the period between the winter solstice (about 21 December) and the spring equinox (about 21 March). However, snows deep enough to cause deer to move to winter range can come as early as the first of November and may not melt to allow the deer to return to their summer range until

On northern parts of their range, whitetails seasonally migrate, leaving summer feeding and resting areas to concentrate in traditional winter cover and—if they survive—to return again in spring.

almost the end of April. Whitetails' winters may last almost six months, and during winters of little snow, no seasonal movements may occur.

Winter weather in the whitetail's range varies tremendously from year to year, as does snow depth and temperature. If global warming is occurring, as many predict, we may find that the distribution and abundance of whitetails will change over time. In most of their range, the greatest mortality on whitetails is caused by hunting. During severe winters in the snowbelt, however, losses due to starvation and predation may exceed hunting losses. Some years deer are in their summer range during the hunting season; other years they are en route to their winter range, and some years they are concentrated in their winter yards. The vulnerability to hunters changes accordingly. Vulnerability also changes in different habitats and in varying sizes of blocks of cover. The interaction of weather, hunting, habitat, and deer social structure on different population segments makes the whitetail winter complex and variable.

Differences in the vulnerability of different segments of its population are the main reason for the differences in density and movements in different parts of the whitetail's range. If these differences are understood, the manager can use the information to either help increase or decrease segments of the population by changing the time and place of hunting.

Most states now manage their deer herds by management units. This occurs so that the manager can better regulate the population in smaller areas. A challenge to managers is to set regulations that will keep deer populations within carrying capacity of their range, but to promulgate rules that are simple enough not to discourage deer hunters from hunting. Duck hunting and trout fishing regulations have already become so complex that the number of participants in these sports has declined.

With the exception of populations living at very high densities, white-tailed deer do not have self-limiting mechanisms to control their population growth. Hunting is therefore essential to their management. This book will help everyone interested in white-tailed deer to understand the complexities of the winter ecology of this species and, it is hoped, to allow for better management of this truly amazing species.

— *Orrin J. Rongstad*
Emeritus Professor
University of Wisconsin
Department of Wildlife Ecology

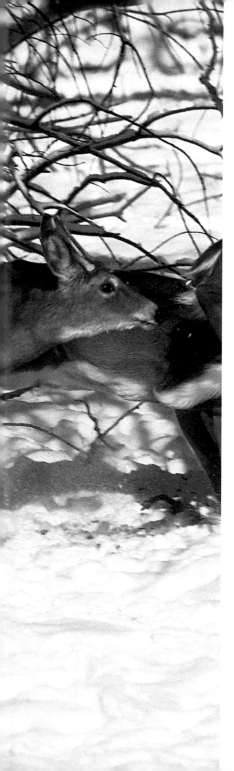

INTRODUCTION

Because events that occur throughout the year of the white-tailed deer are so closely intertwined, it's impossible for me to completely separate the seasons when discussing the behavior of these fascinating creatures. What a whitetail experiences, favorably or otherwise, and how it adjusts, physiologically and behaviorally during any given season, will have a direct bearing upon its behavior, reproductive success, general well-being, and even its chances of surviving during the months ahead. This is especially true for whitetails living at the northern extremity of their geographic range, where the species' very existence is precarious and largely dependent upon the outcome of the winter season.

In the Northern Hemisphere, the whitetail's cyclic rhythms in physiology, metabolism, coat molt, reproduction, and general behavior are closely regulated by, or cued to, the changing amount of daylight, or "photoperiod." The shortening day

Along their winter migration trails, whitetails face increased peril from predators and must remain alert and ready to flee to safety.

length in autumn triggers a complex chain of physiological events that lead to the whitetail's growth of a thick insulative winter coat, the accumulation of heavy fat deposits, breeding initiation, and various other changes in behavior, all of which enhance the species' prospects for surviving the bleak winter season. In the North, especially, the timing of the whitetail's breeding is strictly regulated by decreasing photoperiod, ensuring that fawn births occur on schedule in spring and summer when food and cover conditions are most favorable for their survival.

Today, the whitetail is at home in many north-temperate to tropical environments, ranging from near tree line in southern Canada into the Amazon rain forests of South America. Indeed, few other large mammals demonstrate such extreme adaptiveness or have the inherent ability to cope with such widely ranging ecological conditions.

Obviously, whitetails that live near the equator are not subjected to drastic seasonal changes in photoperiod and therefore do not experience the climatic adversity associated with the winter season. As a result, whitetails found near the equator have evolved totally different lifestyles, ones generally not exhibiting the strict seasonal rhythms demonstrated by the those members of the species living farther northward.

Whitetails inhabiting tropical and neotropical ranges are not subjected to the pressures of climatic change. Consequently, they've evolved different survival strategies than those exhibited by deer in northern climes.

Where snow seasonally blankets deer range, food shortages place severe selective pressure on whitetails. Deer adept at finding food in winter stand the best chances of surviving and contributing progeny to the herd.

Whitetail densities have actually increased in northern areas where agricultural crops are available as winter supplements to an otherwise meager winter diet.

Even within the continental United States, however, due to varying environmental pressures and resultant selective forces, the seasonal biological needs and behavior of whitetails, especially in winter, differ rather dramatically from north to south. Although the winter season may not be particularly tough on deer in southern parts of the United States, winter is still a sinister grim reaper in northern states where the combination of prolonged cold weather, deep snow cover, inadequate shelter, and poor food conditions frequently contribute to extreme hardship for whitetails.

On portions of the northern deer range, the annual winter death toll on whitetails may even exceed that of the legal harvest by hunters. In the Upper Great Lakes region and in the northeastern U.S., hundreds of thousands of whitetails may perish from the combined effects of malnutrition and predation during an extremely stressful winter.

In the South, occasional droughts, floods, or other unusual weather patterns that cause poor autumn or winter food conditions can periodically set the stage for sizeable malnutrition-related losses of whitetails during the winter season. But pressures wrought by climatic conditions in the South do not begin to compare to the severity of those acting on northern deer populations.

In the North, selective pressures have favored whitetail traits that are closely linked to rhythmic, often abrupt, seasonal fluctuations in the availability of food and shelter. As one progresses northward, more and more of the whitetail's lifetime is devoted to preparing for, enduring, or recovering from the stressful winter season.

How a northern whitetail behaves during winter, and whether or not it survives, will hinge heavily upon when it was born, how well it was nourished and grew during summer, the level of fatness it achieved during autumn, and the severity of the winter season relative to the availability of food and shelter.

Seasonal variations in climate and food availability set the biological pace for deer on northern range. These natural rhythmic phenomena and the day-length cycle govern whitetails' physiological condition and, thus, their breeding and birthing schedules.

Whitetails living in northern regions where they are cold-stressed and burdened with heavy snow cover must prepare in advance for the perilous winter season. During winter they must become ultra-energy-conservative in order to survive. Their adaptive traits for winter survival include an array of timely physiological changes, greatly reduced movement activity, shelter-seeking behavior (yarding, which sometimes requires lengthy migration), intense socialization, and a host of other behavioral adjustments. These adaptive changes permit them to better cope with the pending negative energy balance and to minimize the dangers that hungry predators present.

Northern whitetails deviating greatly from these highly adaptive adjustments—generated through centuries of ancestral response to environmental stress—are less likely to survive and perpetuate alternate patterns not conducive to surviving the limitations imposed by the harsh winter season.

For obvious reasons, selective pressures imposed by cold weather and snow cover are less operative in the South. There even late-born, small, and weak deer stand a good chance of surviving the comparatively mild and typically brief periods of winter.

I consider myself fortunate to have literally lived with whitetails on northern range through many winters. Commencing with my studies in 1961, I watched whitetails struggle to cope with unbelievable winter stress, especially as it prevails along the south shore of Lake Superior. I watched hundreds of whitetails die there, but I always marveled at the fact that somehow, almost miraculously, so many could survive such hardship and deprivation. Believe me, this animal we call the whitetail is as opportunistic as any of God's creatures, and far more resourceful than most.

In the Upper Great Lakes region, the 1960s and early 1970s were lean years for whitetails. Deer populations plummeted, and state wildlife management agencies were blamed for the deer herd's demise. In those days, one didn't boast too loudly in public about being a game biologist; it was a time when much of the hunting public pledged to support state wildlife biologists with a rope. I damned that ignorant segment of the public for not being able to understand the obvious ecological relationships that were involved.

The problem in those days was really so simple— Mother Nature was just doing her thing. Forest cover had matured; the amount of good food available for deer had decreased; there were just too many deer mouths to feed; and we experienced a series of especially severe winters. At the time, it really didn't matter, of course, what the cause—hunting, predators, accidents or malnutrition—a large percentage of the autumn deer herd, including many unborn fawns, would not survive to experience the freshness of another spring.

Since those earlier years, things have changed. For one thing, my snowshoeing pace has strangely shortened. But whitetails also seem to have changed much in that very short time, having learned to take advantage of human progress. Whitetail numbers have risen sharply in recent years— too sharply in many areas, where they've attained "pest" status. And in some cases

they seem to have become almost totally dependent upon humans, in one way or another, for sustenance during the winter season.

I am admittedly biased in my coverage of the whitetail's life during winter. My perspective is that of a northerner. I come from an area where winters are normally harsh, with five or more months of cold weather and snow cover the annual norm. Through more than 30 years of study in northern Michigan, I've come to better understand how whitetails cope with winter adversity. I've gained a very deep respect for the northern subspecies (*Odocoileus virginianus borealis*) in particular, as it struggles to survive against what sometimes appear to be overwhelming odds.

For the reader that has never experienced a truly harsh whitetail winter, who has not trudged the maze of manure-packed deer trails that crisscross a cedar swamp deer yard, or who has never read the tell-tale signs left behind by this amazing creature as it strives to hang on while not becoming food for others that share its hostile winter world, be my guest. I'll do my best to lead you through the whitetail's winter as I and many other dedicated scientists have come to know it.

WHITETAIL EVOLUTION AND BERGMANN'S RULE

The origin of the deer family, Cervidae, is still somewhat obscure. We assume that true antlered cervids first appeared in Eurasia some 20 million years ago and entered North America via a land bridge that once linked present-day Alaska with northeastern Siberia. (The bridge finally submerged about 15,500 years ago when glacial melt caused rising sea levels to join the Pacific and Arctic oceans, creating the Bering Strait.) As the climate cooled and glaciers formed, this ancestral cervid was gradually pushed southward. It reached the continental United States about four million years ago and later entered South America over the Pliocene land bridge.

The genus *Odocoileus,* which includes the whitetail, blacktail, and mule deer, is regarded as an American development. The white-tailed deer *(Odocoileus virginianus)* as we know it today is considered to be the ancestral form.

Size dissimilarity among whitetail subspecies is an adaptation to climatic extremes. Large deer, like this magnificent northern whitetail buck, are physically better equipped to conserve heat.

The whitetail's inherent ability to adapt to a variety of geographical conditions has allowed it to flourish and expand its range in a diverse array of habitats.

According to former Michigan State University professor Rollin H. Baker: "In the Pleistocene era, starting about one million years ago, New World cervids, including the whitetail, shared both forested and open areas with an impressive array of hoofed associates, including mammoths, mastodons, horses, tapirs, peccaries, camelids, pronghorns and bovids. Only nine cervid genera, one pronghorn and nine bovid genera—plus a few neotropical tapirs, camelids (llamas and allies), and peccaries—survived the postglacial ordeals and inhabit the Western Hemisphere today. The rest of the great assemblage of ice age ungulates has disappeared, and the reasons why are in dispute."

Some 20,000 years ago, a multitude of large mammals—some of gigantic proportions—lived not far south of the massive ice sheets that blanketed nearly all of Canada and northern portions of the United States. Among this multitude of life, the diversity of large ungulates devouring copious amounts

of vegetative materials must have been impressive.

As noted by Baker and other prominent scientists, the reasons for the disappearance of so many large species since the ice age are unknown. There are two chief theories. According to one theory, the species that vanished were exterminated by human hunters. According to the other, the species that vanished were those unable to adapt to the rapidly changing environment. Both theories have their weaknesses.

Regardless, the hardy whitetail has endured. It has outlived many of its former associates and even deadly enemies such as the fierce saber-toothed tiger, the giant short-faced bear, and the dire wolf. Furthermore, not only did the white-tailed deer adapt and survive the perilous post-glacial period, but once the massive ice sheets receded sufficiently and the area eventually became vegetated, whitetails promptly extended their range northward.

Noted scientist Valerius Geist of the University of Calgary refers to the white-tailed deer as "a living fossil and an outrageous success because it has not changed much in form—if at all—over millions of years. Not changing, not evolving, and not being disrupted by great ecological changes are the hallmarks of biological success."

Geist points out that one of the whitetail's chief weaknesses is its inability to compete with other ungulates for living-space. Instead, he emphasizes, "The whitetail specializes in opportunism, not contest or competition. During the past 2 million years in the major ice ages, it became a member of an ecologically highly specialized fauna, a fauna that died out at the end of the ice ages, leaving the white-tailed deer as one of the few survivors. In post-glacial times—that is in the past 10,000 years—the whitetail, freed from oppressive competition by specialized herbivores and predation by diverse carnivores, exploded into abundance."

Few whitetails, or for that matter any other herbivore, could have lived in glaciated portions of the Great Lakes region, the Northeast, in the Northern Plains of the United States, or in Canada during the ice ages. In other words, although whitetails have lived in the southern United States for at least the past million years, they've only re-occupied much of their current northern range during the past few thousand years. In the past 100 years or so, due largely to man's alteration of natural habitats (and probably to the reduction in the numbers of natural predators), the whitetail has pushed even farther northward and westward.

Whitetails from one region of the country may look somewhat different than those from another. This is not unexpected, of course, given that the species acclimates to a wide range of environmental conditions. Differences in body size, general body proportions, coat

Today, whitetails thrive in wilderness settings as well as in areas densely populated with humans. This ability to opportunistically accommodate their surroundings is slowly pushing whitetail range farther north and west.

color, and other physical details are the direct result of exposure and adaptation to contrasting environmental factors. Such geographically adapted subpopulations are considered to be subspecies (races), in that they differ significantly, one from the other.

Currently, taxonomists recognize 30 subspecies of white-tailed deer in North and Central America and eight in South America. Classification is confusing, however, and often debated. This is because the ranges of many subspecies overlap, integration is widespread, and thousands of whitetails have been captured and liberated far beyond the boundaries of their normal subspecific ranges.

Organized restocking programs were especially popular in the 1930s, 1940s, and 1950s, when many southern states attempted to replenish deer herds that had been depleted during the 1800s. Most translocated deer came from Wisconsin, Michigan, North Carolina, and Texas. Nearly every state in the Southeast received some deer from outside sources, and most of these transplanted deer were subspecies not native to the area where they were released.

Evidence derived from sophisticated mitochondrial DNA analysis suggests, however, that present deer populations in the southeastern U.S. are primarily descended from native herds, not from relocated deer.

Even so, other scientists argue that the genetic origins of certain southern deer herds are unknown and question whether the deer are native subspecies, introduced subspecies, or hybrids of subspecies.

Although some subspecies may differ only in subtle facial, body, and tail markings and colorations, others may differ greatly in body size. The largest subspecies, which include the northern woodland *(O. v. borealis)*, Dakota *(O. v. dacotensis)*, and northwest *(O. v. ochrorous)* whitetails, inhabit the northern United States

Due to a plethora of translocation programs earlier in this century, populations of whitetails in the southeastern United States became genetically suspect. Recent DNA analyses, however, indicate present populations are those of native subspecies.

While tropical subspecies of whitetails may weigh no more than 40 or 50 pounds, northern subspecies may weigh up to 400 pounds. The largest-bodied whitetails, males of which also grow the largest antlers, are found on the northern extremes of whitetail range.

and Canada. These deer stand about 40 inches at the shoulder, and males can weigh up to 400 pounds. In contrast, the smallest whitetails tend to come from warmer, southerly climates. For example, the Margarita Island subspecies *(O. v. margaritae)* that lives off the coast of Venezuela may weigh less than 40 pounds at maturity.

This geographic trend in body size—largest in the north, smallest near the equator, with intermediate sizes occurring at mid-latitudes—is also seen in other mammals and is referred to as Bergmann's Rule, after the scientist who first observed and described the phenomenon. This relationship of body size to latitude is of interest to deer hunters because body size and antler size generally go together. That is, the largest-bodied bucks generally grow the largest antlers and tend to come from northern portions of the whitetail's geographic range.

More importantly, the biological manifestation of Bergmann's Rule has special survival value for deer in that it permits them to better cope with extreme, unfavorable temperatures. Since a large body has less surface area in relation to total body mass, a large-bodied deer retains body heat more efficiently than does a small-bodied deer. Such an energy-conserving advantage could mean the difference between life and death for northern whitetails faced with prolonged exposure to periods of sub-zero temperatures, periods often accompanied by limited supplies of food of low nutritive value. Conversely, small-bodied deer living in areas of hot weather are better able to dissipate surplus heat and maintain body temperature equilibrium.

Although genetic factors largely account for the body size differences articulated in Bergmann's Rule, prevailing environmental conditions also play a vital role. The large northern subspecies of whitetails have the innate ability to grow to large size, but they must be born on schedule and be well nourished in order to do so.

Regardless of their birth date, fawns that are malnourished during summer and autumn are not likely to achieve their maximum growth potential prior to facing their first stressful winter season, which decreases their prospects for survival. Even if stunted fawns do survive their first winter, they seldom demonstrate compensatory growth later in life, especially if subjected to continued dietary deficiencies; most grow up to be undersized adults.

The large *borealis* subspecies whose members live on the rich farmlands of the Midwest probably demonstrate Bergmann's Rule most clearly. While occurring at low to moderate densities throughout Indiana, Illinois, Ohio, southern Michigan, and southern Wisconsin, these

The Rocky Mountains, native domain of the mule deer, sees more and more whitetails in its ridges and valleys each year. Western expansion of the whitetail's range has some biologists worried that mule deer numbers will diminish as a result.

whitetails enjoy rich forage year-round and face winter weather of only moderate severity. Given such ideal nutrition, minimal social stress, and favorable climate, even the late-born farmland fawns stand a good chance of achieving their maximum growth potential at adult age.

In the Upper Great Lakes region and in the Northeast, however, not all whitetails grow to their large size potential. Although unusually small deer sometimes are the result of late births, poor nutrition is more commonly the cause of poor growth among northern deer. In the North, strong selective pressures prevail that favor physical fitness, because the harsh winter climate there normally dictates deer welfare and tends to weed-out the small, the weak, and the genetically inferior.

Usually, the frequent occurrence of smaller-than-normal deer on northern range is symptomatic of dietary problems due either to soil infertility or, more commonly, depletion of preferred

(more nutritious) plants due to excessive foraging by overly abundant deer. In either case, the stunted-deer phenomenon sends a clear message that all is not well with the local northern deer herd and that populations are too high for the food resources available. Given such dietary shortage, Bergmann's Rule can not operate to its fullest extent, and many small, unhealthy deer are likely to succumb to malnutrition or fall victim to predators, even during those winters of only moderate severity.

The importance of Bergmann's Rule transcends far beyond mere academic interest. For those whitetails normally subjected to harsh winter climates, achieving maximal body growth prior to winter is crucial to their future reproductive success and, ultimately, to their very existence.

Since the whitetail sexes differ in many aspects of their life history, including their growth rates and ultimate body size at maturity—and demonstrate what

For whitetails on northern range, attaining maximum growth and fat deposits during spring and summer are essential. The whitetails' subsequent reproductive success requires building metabolic reserves to carry deer through months of cold and food deprivation.

scientists refer to as "resource partitioning" or "niche separation" of the sexes—this entire issue of deer welfare and Bergmann's Rule becomes rather complex. In some cases, social factors may impact whitetail welfare just about as effectively as does nutrition.

In the words of whitetail research scientist Dale McCullough: "Resource partitioning between the sexes in white-tailed deer adds a new dimension to the role of social behavior as it relates the animal to its environment."

On a seasonal basis, if bucks differ from does in their use of space, food, and cover resources, whitetail habitat-management and harvest-management considerations take on an entirely new level of complexity. Habitat manipulations that benefit female deer might not necessarily equally benefit bucks or sometimes might even be detrimental to bucks. Likewise, harvest strategies that inflict unnatural patterns of mortality (such as bucks-only shooting) and create herds with abnormal sex and age composition—thereby altering important aspects of the whitetail's social environment—could affect the welfare of one sex, favorably or otherwise, more so than the other. Unfortunately, the inter-relationships involved in Bergmann's Rule, niche separation of the sexes, and white-tailed deer herd and habitat management have not been thoroughly investigated and currently are only poorly understood.

Whitetail bucks remain separate from does most of the year, utilizing different habitat within the same range occupied by the female component of the herd.

PHYSIOLOGICAL ADJUSTMENTS

In winter the whitetail's coat consists of stiff hollow guard hairs, which are quite long and dark in color, and a very fine but deeper, wooly underfur. The thickness of this protective coat varies appreciably from one part of the whitetail's body to another, providing better covering on the animal's back and sides than on the lower portions of its legs. Although the guard hairs tend to absorb some solar radiation because of their dark color, it is the extreme density of the underfur that makes the whitetail's winter pelage so highly insulative.

During times of extreme cold, whitetails have the ability to increase the insulative properties of their pelage even more by contracting skin muscles attached to the hair shafts, causing the hair to stand erect. This process, called "piloerection," helps to trap air near the skin surface, thereby increasing the thickness of the insulative layer.

In winter, bucks enter a critical period of metabolic demand with depleted body reserves. During the rut, many bucks actually lose weight and become physically weakened.

The cold temperatures, increased wind chill, snow cover, and food deprivation that normally accompany northern winters create a certain amount of hardship for all wildlife. In order to survive, animals must make certain adjustments to maintain metabolism—the fire of life that smolders in every living creature. Maintenance of a basal level of metabolism spells the difference between life and death, and that life-giving fire is easily extinguished when fuel, in the form of nutritious food, is in short supply.

One of the basic functions of metabolism is to maintain body temperature within a range tolerable to the species. As noted by Helenette Silver, a pioneer researcher of white-tailed deer nutrition, "Life in motion—growth, digestion of food, reproduction—and the energy for all this is provided by the fire of life. Individual fires die down or flare up as circumstances dictate, but they can never be extinguished so long as life persists."

For most northern whitetails, a reduction in the availability of nutritious food during winter is a certainty. At the same time, cold-stress saps more of their body heat, and accumulating snow depths make travel difficult and energetically costly. Over the course of winter, a less then favorable set of circumstances arises: a fuel shortage wherein the whitetails' fat reserves are depleted and the woody browse they consume provides insufficient fuel to meet demands imposed by the stressful season. Invariably, the result is a negative energy balance and, ultimately, weight loss.

Some weight loss among whitetails wintering on northern range seems inevitable. Therefore, the individual's survival prospects will hinge heavily upon the amount of reserve fat it builds prior to winter and the rate at which that reserve is burned during winter. In order to survive while on a negative energy balance, the whitetail must become a master at conserving energy (and simultaneously avoid hungry predators).

When cold temperatures and wind chill become severe, whitetails in northern habitats burn more calories in daily maintenance than they take in as food, requiring deer to live on accumulated body reserves.

The whitetail's cost of living is high during winter. For those individuals that have not entered winter in a physically well developed and fattened condition, or even for fattened animals that deplete their energy reserves before spring brings about renewed food sources, the prospects for surviving a tough winter are especially dismal.

Whitetails currently living on northern range are the progeny of ancestral stock that endured thousands of hard winters. They carry with them certain adaptations and inherited traits involving some rather mysterious physiological and behavioral adjustments that ameliorate the adverse effects of the winter season.

As the famous ecologist Paul Errington proclaimed many years ago, "…the one common propensity of animals is to live if they can and die if they must." But the whitetail is not one to readily relinquish its grip on life. In winter, when the going gets tough, the northern whitetail seems to get just that much tougher.

Whitetail's that are normally subjected to harsh winter weather unconsciously begin to prepare for winter's blast long in advance. Rhythmic internal changes in body function, determined by the change of seasons and declining photoperiod, and mediated through actions of the tiny pineal gland, trigger changes in hormone production that induce coat molt and

prompt fattening. These are obligatory events in that they come about pretty much on schedule annually, even if nutrition is less than favorable or weather conditions are unseasonable. And as the winter season progresses, other physiological and behavioral adjustments also kick in, in a reasonably timely fashion, to enhance the whitetail's prospects for survival, even during the most bitter of winters.

Physiological and behavioral adjustments to harsh weather are inherited adaptations that northern subspecies have acquired from countless generations of whitetail predecessors.

The whitetail's insulative coat changes seasonally. The timing of the spring and fall molts are controlled by various factors, including environmental cues, hormonal production, sex, and age.

COAT MOLT

Functionally, seasonal changes in the coloration and thickness of the whitetail's pelage are critically important because they provide camouflage for predator defense and permit the animal to better meet seasonally changing demands for thermoregulation. Coloration of the adult whitetail's winter coat, which young-of-the-year achieve soon after weaning, usually in September or early October, will vary somewhat from one part of the country to the next. In general, because natural selection favors a coat color that blends in well with the environment, deer living in the humid forested areas of the eastern United States and Canada will have slightly darker coats, whereas deer with pale-colored coats tend to inhabit the dry grasslands of western and southwestern North America.

According to George A. Bubenik, who has done extensive research on cervid physiology at the University of Guelph, in Ontario, the whitetail's pineal gland produces a hormone called melatonin, which, at dusk, is increasingly released into the blood. Bubenik says, "When the days begin to lengthen after the winter solstice, the body receives a little less melatonin each day. The cumulative effect is a lower level of melatonin in the bloodstream. This initiates the spring molt—but not directly. The fluctuation of melatonin levels modifies the secretion of the pituitary hormone prolactin. It is the level of prolactin—rising in the spring, peaking at the summer solstice in June, and falling until the dark night of the winter solstice—that ultimately triggers the molt."

Bubenik is quick to caution, however, that other hormones may also affect the timing of the fall molt. He also suggests that the completeness of the autumn coat molt is somewhat temperature-dependent in that the undercoat does not commence growing until the ambient temperature drops. An animal's sex, age, reproductive status, level of nutrition, and probably numerous other factors will also interact to set the precise timing of an individual deer's coat molt.

The pelage of adult deer is composed of four recognizably different hair types: large guard hairs, which are scattered over the body; intermediate guard hairs, which form the bulk of the pelage; mane-type hairs, which are restricted to areas around the rump and tail; and wooly underhairs, which constitute the undercoat of the animal.

The whitetail's red summer coat has no underfur, only relatively thin, short guard hairs, and its ears, which may serve as radiators, have an especially sparse hair covering. Hence, the lightweight summer pelage permits surplus body heat to dissipate readily during hot weather.

The insulative waterproof coat of whitetail deer protects them from heat loss due to exposure to wet snow, freezing rain, and ravaging winter winds.

If it were not for the waterproof quality of the whitetail's pelage, however, the hair would lose its insulating properties when wet. As noted by Bubenik, sebaceous glands in the whitetail's skin manufacture a water-repellent oil (sebum) that slowly leaks onto the skin surface and coats the hair filaments, keeping both the hair and skin soft, elastic, and waterproof.

We often observe that nursing does keep their red summer coats longer than does that fail to raise fawns. One reason for this difference is chemistry. Prolactin, "the hormone from the pituitary gland that, when declining and acting with other hormones," says Bubenik, "signals the body to produce the winter coat, is also the hormone that regulates lactation. The high level of prolactin associated with milk production is at odds with the low level associated with hair growth. The other reason is energy. Both processes drain the doe's energy reserves, and she cannot accomplish both at once."

Molting, a process that averages about three weeks in duration, is metabolically expensive. The four to five pounds of hair produced by the average adult deer each season requires a diet especially high in protein. And according to Bubenik, "The drain on energy and protein reserves deer experience during the molt explains why animals in good physical condition molt first—before weak bucks and late-born fawns as well as before lactating does. In fact, a late onset of the development of wooly fur is a better (and easier-to-read) indicator of under-nourishment than the estimation of integumental fat."

Obviously, in many respects, molting and accumulating heavy fat reserves go hand in hand; both occur at about the same time of the year and are hormonally driven, being largely dependent upon a natural decline in prolactin production. Both events also require an excellent diet high in protein and digestible energy. Come autumn, deer still wearing red—most likely nursing does and fawns—probably don't have much body fat, but the ones already molted into their brown-gray winter coat—more likely adult bucks—may already possess heavy fat deposits around their intestines and kidneys.

FAT ACCUMULATION

By late July, when adult bucks complete most of their new antler growth and replenish body tissues that had been depleted during the previous winter and rutting season, their nutritional demands for basic body maintenance are actually quite minimal. Except in some arid southern environments, the late summer to early autumn period preceding the rut is normally a good time of year for the mature whitetail buck. Environ-mental stress is generally minimal, while nutrition is

Due to metabolic demands of lactation and growth, respectively, does and their fawns molt into their winter coats later than non-nursing does, and bucks and yearling whitetails.

optimal. From this time until the ensuing rut, a good portion of the mature buck's energy intake will be channeled into building fat reserves necessary to meet the taxing demands associated with forming the autumn dominance-hierarchy and with breeding.

In many ways, however, the buck's annual fat cycle seems maladaptive. A buck prepares himself almost totally for mating and siring future offspring, but holds very little energy in reserve for winter survival. The strenuous autumn rut drains the buck of his fat stores. He'll probably lose 20 to 25 percent of his peak autumn body weight during the coarse of the breeding season, leaving him quite lean and seemingly very vulnerable to the climatic stress and nutritional shortage that winter is sure to bring. In that regard, one must wonder if the mature buck does not possess other special, poorly understood capabilities that more than offset such an otherwise seemingly suicidal tendency.

As implied previously, adult does within the same herd may vary considerably in their degree of fatness when winter starts, depending largely upon their reproductive history. Given good range conditions, favorable weather, and ample forage, mature does that have not been burdened with nursing fawns the previous season tend to replenish their body reserves well in advance of the rut. More than likely, they'll enter winter

hog-fat and well-prepared. On the other hand, those does that have raised fawns may not be quite so well-off at the start of winter, especially if they gave birth to fawns late in the season, were burdened with nursing twins or triplets, or for some other reason experienced poor nutrition during the autumn period.

Of all age-classes of deer, young-of-the-year (fawns) find themselves in greatest jeopardy because they must consume enough nutrients to maximize their growth prior to winter and simultaneously lay away adequate fat stores for reserve energy. It is essential for northern whitetail to be well prepared in case Arctic blasts arrive unusually early. So, being born on schedule—at an optimal time to be prepared for winter—is critically important. Late-born individuals are seriously disadvantaged.

Given favorable circumstances, northern male whitetails weighing only six to seven pounds at birth in late May or early June can easily attain a weight in excess of 100 pounds by six months of age in early December, when they normally reach their maximum pre-winter size. (Female fawns will generally run 10 to 15 percent lighter.) However, in order to do so, the young whitetail's level of nutrition must be optimal throughout the nursing and post-weaning periods. Many factors, including poor maternal nutrition, littermate

Rut-stressed bucks may lose all or most of the fat they accumulated prior to autumn. For them, conserving energy through the course of the ensuing winter season will be especially critical.

competition, low soil fertility, overbrowsed range, drought, early snow cover, and so forth, may prevent these young deer from reaching their full potential skeletal size and degree of fatness prior to onset of winter.

Research conducted at the Cusino Wildlife Research Station in Upper Michigan revealed that fawns on restricted diets during October and November were considerably smaller and leaner at the start of winter than fawns provided with unlimited, high-quality feed during the same period (which, of course, in itself, was not really unexpected). Considering their poor growth, however, fawns on marginal or poor diets still accumulated surprisingly large fat stores. We concluded, therefore, that fat accumulation among northern deer is predominantly an obligatory process under hormonal control, meaning that undernourished young animals will sacrifice growth, if necessary, in order to build some fat reserves in preparation for winter.

From a wildlife manager's perspective, then, the occurrence of fat fawns during the late autumn period may not necessarily signify good range conditions for deer. Healthy fawns will be skeletally large, in addition to being fat, whereas malnourished fawns may be fairly fat, but stunted in skeletal growth.

Young animals require diets containing an adequate amount of protein, in addition to other essential nutrients, for proper growth. However, the Cusino investigations revealed that a protein-rich diet is not really vital to fawns in autumn. However, even a relatively small energy deficiency in the diet can slow their growth rate and decrease their level of fatness. Regardless of their diet, female fawns normally accumulated more fat than males, suggesting that male reproductive hormones are also somehow involved and probably account, even in young deer, for the disparity of fat stored between the sexes (possibly a factor affecting their overwinter survival rates).

The rut sometimes continues into early winter. Until it is completed, mature bucks remain solitary and challenge other bucks for mating privileges with estrous does.

METABOLISM

The first blasts of winter bring about a host of unfavorable changes for whitetails not yet acclimated to the stresses of the new season. Most importantly, the freezing temperatures and snow cover that characterize early winter will necessitate a change in the whitetail's diet. In many northern areas, this equates to a shift from eating succulent, highly nutritious herbaceous forage to subsistence upon less-nourishing woody browse— even the best of which is comparatively low in protein, digestible energy, and other essential dietary constituents.

Although healthy whitetails are fairly well prepared for winter, being heavily insulated and laden with fat, cold-stress still causes discomfort. In conjunction with mounting snow depths that cover nourishing foods and impair travel, the chill of winter prompts deer to seek protective dense conifer cover in order to minimize body heat loss and to reduce the threat from predators. This shelter-seeking tendency, commonly demonstrated by whitetails throughout their northern range and referred to as "yarding," is rather obvious, but less apparent physiological changes also take place during this initial period of winter acclimation.

When initially adjusting to winter weather, whitetails tend to be quite active. They travel about a great deal, moving from their traditional, poorly sheltered summer range to concentrate in the best protective cover available. Some late breeding may also occur during early winter. These activities only add extra demands to an already energetically expensive time for whitetails, especially if bucks strange to one another (those outside the dominance-hierarchy established on summer range where bucks are familiar with one another's prowess) vie for such late-season mating privileges. As a result, deer tend to eat a lot during this period of seasonal adjustment, presumably to offset the high metabolic requirements associated with their active lifestyle. But, in some instances, whitetails may exhibit appreciable weight loss even before the stressful winter season really gets under way.

As winter progresses, however, and as they gradually acclimate to the season, whitetails shift into low gear, metabolically speaking. Instead of accelerating body heat production to compensate for cold exposure, the whitetail's metabolic rate actually declines as the deer become extremely miserly in regard to their energy expenditure.

Obviously, whitetails do not sleep out the winter and they do not reduce their body temperature any signifi-cant degree. According to biologist Helenette Silver, though, whitetails do show sharply reduced thyroid

When the rut is completed, bucks as well as does, fawns and yearlings undergo a short period of binge feeding to lay on as much fat as possible prior to the onset of winter.

Injuries sustained by bucks fighting during the rut require additional outlays of energy for healing. Serious injuries thus exacerbate metabolic demands for normal body maintenance at the onset of winter.

function and cut their metabolic rate by about half in winter. By mid-winter, acclimated whitetails adopt a unique form of dormancy, or semi-hibernation, quite similar in many respects to that demonstrated by the black bear. In the process, the deer become quite resistant to nutritional shortage and climatic stress.

This reduction in metabolic rate doesn't mean that deer need less heat to counteract cold. According to Silver, "If their basal requirements for merely living decrease even as their requirements for combating cold increase, one need tends to balance out the other, and they wind up having to produce about the same amount of heat winter and summer. It takes a lot of strain off the furnace."

Since metabolism is the sum of all physical and chemical activity involved in the production or maintenance of living tissue, the deer's reduced metabolic rate in winter is reflected in its food consumption, its rate of growth, its heart rate, its movement activity, and as emphasized by Silver, "...probably every area of its existence. And this indeed, is the case. In the coldest part of the year our deer voluntarily reduce their food intake, they apparently stop growing and lose weight, their heart rate decreases, and they become much less active. Life goes on at a lower level in all areas."

The whitetail's adaptive system of seasonally changing physiology is not infallible, however, and does not guarantee the overwinter survival of all deer—not even for those animals that enter winter physically fit and well prepared.

Toward the end of winter, as the hours of daylight increase, the wintering whitetail's physiology and behavior changes markedly. In Upper Michigan, deer of both sexes and all ages become much more active after mid-March and, given the opportunity, demonstrate steadily rising food consumption. Although the concurrent physiological changes are poorly understood, the rise in activity is presumably associated with an increase in thyroid function and rising metabolism. Depending upon prevailing temperatures and snow conditions, deer sometimes experience extremely exhausting travel conditions at spring break-up. This makes a bad situation even worse. If these unfavorable conditions are prolonged, many fat-depleted and weakened deer, unable to meet their rising energy requirements, may then perish from malnutrition.

BEHAVIORAL ADJUSTMENTS

Seasonal rhythms in the behavior of white-tailed deer are influenced by a host of environmental factors. Due to differing climatic conditions during winter, whitetails living in northern regions behave much differently than those living in milder southern climates. But even in the north, and even over the distance of only a few miles, profound differences can sometimes be seen in the whitetail's behavioral strategies for winter survival.

There are many trade-offs—involving nutrition, shelter, and predator risk—in the whitetail's tactical bid for winter survival. But it's as though the stressed whitetail possessed its own sophisticated computer system necessary to calculate energy cost-benefit ratios, predict potential predator risks, and make the best judgments possible in order to survive. It's this uncanny ability to adjust to prevailing and constantly changing circumstances that largely accounts for, between or within regions and over time, different behavioral traits exhibited by whitetails. And it's this behavioral flexibility that allows the species to survive near the northern limits of its geographic range even when it is confronted with unbelievably harsh winter conditions. We have here an animal that is an expert in opportunism.

In any given area during winter, the individual whitetail's behavior will depend upon its sex and age, upon how well it grew and fattened prior to the onset of cold weather, and upon the amount of environmental stress imposed by the season. Prevailing temperatures, wind conditions, and the depth and character of the snowpack—relative to the distribution and availability of protective cover and quality food—will interact to largely govern the whitetail's distribution, movement activity, and daily routine during winter.

Whitetails living in southern states seldom lack adequate cover and can usually find relief from brief periods of adverse weather within their normal home range. In effect, southern whitetails are non-migratory. They spend their entire life within a relatively small area. In fact, in many areas of the South, spring flooding or droughty weather during summer pose a far greater threat to deer welfare than does the coolness of the winter season.

In the north, however, protection from cold weather and deep snow becomes critically important. In many northern regions, deer vacate vast areas of their summer range and sometimes migrate long distances to reach traditional wintering grounds that are dominated by dense conifers. The cover these trees furnish provides deer physical comfort and safety from marauding predators.

SHELTER REQUIREMENTS

The shelter requirements of whitetails in northern regions tend to be quite variable, however, depending largely upon the degree and

In the southern parts of its range, the whitetail enjoys a relatively easy lifestyle free from the adverse effects of harsh winters and inadequate vegetative cover.

As winter progresses and the rut comes to a close, bucks once again become gregarious, gathering in fraternal social groups apart from does and fawns.

During mild winters or when food availability remains high and snow depths do not restrict whitetail movements, deer may not migrate to yarding areas. Instead, they may remain dispersed on summer ranges.

duration of cold-stress and snow cover, which may vary considerably from one year to next, even within the same area. Therefore, not all conifer forests provide adequate shelter for deer every winter, especially where winters are normally severe, prolonged, and characterized by heavy snow accumulations.

On the other hand, shelter requirements may not be so stringent for whitetails living only short distances away, where snowfall may be less. In some of these low-snowfall zones, whitetails may remain quite loosely yarded and well dispersed throughout winter, or the deer may even remain on their summer ranges far from their traditional wintering grounds.

Throughout the Upper Great Lakes region and in the Northeast, only a relatively small portion (probably only about 10 percent) of the total deer range will support whitetails during most winters. Especially during severe winters, large numbers of deer—numbers that far surpass the capacity of the habitat to support healthy deer—tend to congregate on preferred winter range, which frequently results in heavy starvation losses. Consequently, in those areas of heavy annual snowfall, poor winter habitat produces the proverbial survival bottle-neck that dictates deer welfare and determines how many deer will replenish the summer range come spring. Hence, where winter habitat is poor and winters are tough, deer tend to live at fairly low densities (below carrying capacity) on their summer range.

Lowland areas of mature northern white cedar, balsam fir, white, black, and red spruce, along with hemlock, when available in fairly large and uniform stands with dense canopy closure, provide the best cover for wintering whitetails. Such cover may attract deer densities of several hundred per square mile in winter. However, upland hemlock-hardwood, jack pine, white pine, and even red pine provide adequate shelter where weather isn't so severe.

In the Adirondacks of New York, a mountain area characterized by cold climate, deep snow, and a northern forest, the principal wintering areas are evergreen swamps. In central New York, however, where the climate is milder and snowfall less, there is little conifer cover available for deer. There, deer concentrate on steep south and southeast slopes during winter, irrespective of the vegetative type, just as they do central Vermont.

In sparsely forested areas such as in the northern plains, isolated marshes, wooded draws, and brushy stream bottoms serve as wintering cover for whitetails, provided a good food source is available nearby.

Food availability can be an important factor in determining where deer will and won't live during winter. Whitetails seek heavy cover that provides them

The abundance and quality of winter foods is an important factor in determining wintering areas for whitetails. Prime winter habitat will also include thick cover for protection from the elements and from predators.

maximum physical comfort, but in many instances they appear to seek these areas with little regard for the availability of food. There are, however, important trade-offs involved between the amount of energy consumed in food versus the amount spent to obtain it, to avoid predators, and to compensate for cold weather heat-loss.

Deer that subsist solely upon natural browse in winter are generally on a negative energy balance. To reduce their energy expenditure, they must have optimal cover where they can bed comfortably and remain inactive for long periods of time safe from predators.

If highly nutritious food is available, as is the case today where many wintering whitetails feed on agricultural crops such as corn, soybeans, or wheat, or are supplementally fed high-energy grains or specially formulated rations, deer can overwinter successfully even in forested areas that provide poor quality cover.

When deer have ready access to an abundance of high-energy food, the calories gained in feeding easily offset the loss from exposure or travel, even when they are faced with an increased risk from predators. In such cases, the animals can readily afford to sacrifice shelter quality, and in some instances travel fairly long distances to feed, as has been shown to be the case in the northern plains area.

Where winter food and cover are widely separated, deer must make dangerous daily movements to obtain food. In doing so, they place themselves at increased risk to predation and to other mortality factors.

SOCIAL REQUIREMENTS

With extreme cold-stress and mounting snow depths, the importance of social behavior also comes into play in the whitetail's bid for overwinter survival. Deer density, herd sex-age composition, and genetic relationships, all of which determine a deer's social environment, become especially important on northern range. There, hundreds of deer may crowd into traditional deer yards and compete aggressively for the best shelter and the limited food that the area has to offer.

Many of the whitetail's adaptive behavioral traits for winter survival are instinctive, true enough, but some are learned. For northern migratory deer, the young animals must depend upon older, experienced individuals for guidance. Associating with older deer helps the young ones to learn lengthy migratory routes, to locate favorable wintering areas, and learn how to survive in browsed-out yards, often for several months at a time. Having strong social alliances also sometimes buffers the weaker deer from undue social stress, which can mean the difference between life and death, especially for those experiencing their first, and potentially last, harsh northern winter.

Today, throughout most of their range, whitetails' social environments are largely determined by human

hunters and the controlled harvesting of deer during the autumn period. Historically, however, hunting by Native Americans and natural predators played a key role in shaping this prey species' adaptive strategies for winter survival, just as predators still do today in some remote sections of the whitetail's northern range.

I've long contended that the social grouping of related female whitetails and their young, as commonly occurs on northern range during autumn, has numerous but poorly understood adaptive values. The benefits accrued through such socialization, however, seem more important to migratory whitetails on northern range and probably are of less importance to southern deer that are non-migratory.

Because lengthy migration routes followed by northern whitetails are learned, it's essential that young-of-the-year animals, in the event their mothers should die before migration, establish social bonds with adult deer, generally aunts or older sisters that have migratory experience.

It is reasonable to assume that in prehistorical time, or even into the late 18th century, that the reasons for a young whitetail being orphaned were largely due to natural predators or hunting by Native Americans. If so, then premigratory socialization between surviving young deer and older whitetails probably evolved through adaptive selection.

Even today in those areas where many adult female deer are harvested during the autumn hunting seasons, young deer rarely become stranded on summer range during severe winters. General observations suggest that most of these orphaned individuals find compatible adult associations and learn to find suitable habitat in winter, despite the fact that their natal range is far removed from their mothers' ancestral wintering grounds. And since orphaned animals are most likely to achieve compatible associations with adult female relatives, motherless young whitetails tend to use ancestral wintering grounds formerly utilized by their mothers and still used by other female clan members.

(Somewhat different traits were reported by Charles Nixon and his co-workers for whitetails living in intensively farmed portions of Illinois, where forest cover is especially limited. There, about half of the fawns—male and female—dispersed to new range when they were 10 to 12 months old in spring. Having survived the hunting seasons, the fawns then selected wintering sites different from those used by their mothers, because of social relationships the motherless young had developed with unrelated deer during late fall.)

Young-of-the-year whitetails must learn the routes to and from their clan's traditional summer and winter ranges. In the absence of their mothers, related does will lead the way.

It is the onset of very cold weather and not snowfall that stimulates winter migration. Generally, however, deer will migrate to winter range before snow depths begin to hinder their movement.

FALL MIGRATION

Across whitetails' northern range, various factors interact to trigger migrations of deer from their summer to their winter habitats. In Upper Michigan, I've not witnessed any migratory stimulus more timely, more powerful, or more abruptly effective than a raging December blizzard combining the fury of cold, high winds, and blinding snow as it rushes inland off Lake Superior. But not all prewinter migrations of whitetails are so strikingly visible, nor are they always triggered so suddenly.

Most investigations of whitetails' migratory behavior reveal that cold temperatures serve as the primary stimulus prompting deer to seek heavy cover that provides them maximum physical comfort. Mounting snow depths may later act to restrict deer movement to core areas of the best shelter, but, in itself, snowfall seldom seems to cause migration. In fact, most deer migrate to winter yards long before snow becomes deep enough to seriously obstruct their travel.

Even so, the migratory response of deer tends to be quite variable not only between areas, but oftentimes within the same area from one year to the next. The migration dates of deer living in the same area may differ even when deer are presumably simultaneously exposed to the same environmental pressures. The reasons for the

differential migration dates, nevertheless, are not always clear.

Some very interesting documentation of deer migration behavior has been logged by Michael Nelson, David Mech, and Reed Hoskinson while they tracked radio-collared deer in the Superior National Forest of northern Minnesota. Just as I had found in northern Michigan, the Minnesota researchers noted that a high percentage of deer migrated to their winter ranges as temperatures rapidly decreased in November. In some

If cold temperatures moderate during winter migration, deer may return to their summer range. Whitetails may initiate migration several times before they ultimately arrive on their wintering areas.

cases, however, deer showed a delayed response by migrating immediately after a major cold period, when temperatures were actually increasing. In other cases, deer showed no response during several periods of temperature change or did not migrate until December and January when snow depth started to hinder their movements.

Hoskinson and Mech recorded unusually early migrations for one deer, a mature doe, in particular. "On 19 September 1973," the researchers' notes relate, "this animal temporarily left her summer range during the first cold spell and traveled almost 9.6 km (6 miles) toward her wintering area. The minimum temperature on 19 September was 0.6 C, and it dropped below freezing on 20 September for the first time that fall. On 23 September the temperature rose to 15 C, and [the doe] returned to her summer range, having traveled a minimum of 23.3 km (14.5 miles) round trip."

These observations revealed that although a temperature drop may trigger migration, some deer immediately return to their summer range should temperatures increase again. Furthermore, according to the Minnesota biologists: "Although there must be strong advantages to winter grouping when snow is deep, grouping must be maladaptive until that time."

In the Midwest farmland, the amount of snow cover

largely determines deer concentrations. During years with little snow cover, deer frequently remain on their summer ranges all year, just as they do in the northern plains region.

Nutrition may also be an important variable influencing migration date, since, according to Nelson and Mech, "Nutrition may also affect the physiological threshold to thermal changes that induce migration." As in the case of bears, wherein a good food supply tends to delay dormancy, improved nutrition, especially a diet high in energy, may also delay the migration of whitetails from summer to winter range.

Studies conducted by Orrin Rongstad and Tim Lewis on the effects of supplemental feeding on white-tailed deer in northwestern Wisconsin lend support to the theory that a deer's autumn diet can influence its migration date. In their study, wild deer fed highly nutritious pelletized rations during autumn migrated to their traditional wintering cover about two weeks later than other deer that subsisted solely upon natural browse. It's interesting to note, however, despite a continuously available food supply, even the diet-supplemented deer eventually migrated to their traditional wintering areas.

As in the Minnesota studies, Rongstad and Lewis found that fall migration was not always a direct

movement from summer to winter range for most deer and often took 24 to 31 days to complete. Many deer made several trips from summer range toward winter range, but they returned to their summer range as temperatures rose, without ever reaching their wintering grounds. Some deer migrated to a close deer yard, where they remained if the winter was mild, but then moved onto the main deer yard if the winter became harsher. From a practical management consideration, such behavior clearly points out the importance of good food and cover resources for deer peripheral to the core areas of their traditional wintering grounds.

Although group size probably varies a great deal, members of family groups tend to migrate to their winter yards together. It's an interesting aside, though, that neighboring family groups in the Wisconsin study did not always migrate at the same time. In some cases, such difference in migration dates between groups could be explained by the contrasting nutritional status of neighboring family groups in autumn. Moreover, Rongstad and Lewis speculate that the timing of migration is often due to traditional habits, since several of the families they studied consistently migrated early each autumn, even during mild weather.

Adult whitetails are extremely traditional in their range occupation and annually return to the same summer and winter ranges. Some researchers speculate that deer from individual winter yards represent distinct subpopulations of

genetically related individuals, referred to as "demes." Observations that adult deer from each winter yard commonly occupy summer ranges in largely exclusive areas, with minimal overlap among deer from neighboring yards, seem to support such theory. If such were the case, then, a massive die-off of deer within a given yard would greatly reduce deer densities on the associated ancestral summer ranges for many years.

Other studies demonstrate that deer may actually cross paths on their way from summer ranges to traditional wintering grounds. That is, a family of deer may spend the summer close to one deer yard, but then migrate considerable distance to another where they spend the winter. Reasons for such seemingly senseless moves are unknown, but must be ancestral in origin.

Related does and fawns normally band together and migrate to their wintering quarters in groups, but the migratory habits of adult bucks have been poorly documented. Nelson and Mech found that

Deer groups from several summer ranges may share common wintering areas. Traveling in clan groups on their way to winter range, their trails converge as heavily used byways near the winter yard.

Even on winter range where deer become concentrated, their movements are not closely confined to well-used trails until snow depths become restrictive to cross-country travel.

Mutual grooming among deer such as young-of-the-year whitetails is a common behavior on winter yards, where related animals tend to congregate in family groups.

some yearling bucks reunited with their mothers and wintered with the family group, but other observations suggest that yearling bucks join buck groups during autumn and then spend the winter in exclusive male groups. Such differences in young males' behavior may be attributable to differences in deer herd sex-age composition and herd density.

Whether northern bucks migrate to winter yards with other deer, most likely other bucks, or migrate alone, to my knowledge, is unknown. General observations in Upper Michigan suggest that mature dominant bucks, in particular, are reluctant to leave their breeding range and probably are the last to migrate. Regardless of how they travel to the yard, once they arrive on the wintering area, members of fraternal groups likely reunite and spend the winter together, just as they do in non-migratory herds. The impetus here, of course, is that the young buck more than likely forms social bonds with unrelated bucks, because he and other bucks in these groups disperse from their birth ranges at young age. As a result, the young buck may then follow new and probably older associates to new wintering grounds.

Even in the North, not all deer migrate from summer to winter range. Some deer establish summer ranges near deer yards and, during winter, merely shift their centers of activity to take better advantage of heavy cover. About 80 percent of the deer living in central Illinois do not migrate seasonally. In northeastern Wisconsin, Rongstad and Lewis found that about 22 percent of the deer did not migrate. In the Wisconsin study, however, many years of supplemental feeding appeared to alter the ratio of migratory deer; in one area where deer had been fed for over 40 years, 57 percent of the herd were year-round residents.

Many people believe that, prior to the mid-1800s, whitetails were extremely scarce or even absent from much of northern Wisconsin and Upper Michigan, and that deer did not exhibit yarding behavior before the advent of extensive logging and settlement. Others contend that whitetails lived throughout this northern region before the white man arrived (albeit, usually in low numbers), and that deer there have always demonstrated some degree of shelter-seeking and concentration when faced with severe winter weather.

According to William Severinghaus, "There are some deer wintering areas in the Adirondacks (New York) which it is known that deer have used since 1890 or earlier; we know of two locations that were deer yards during the early 1800s and still are used today." Observations such as these indicate that the trait of deer yarding is not totally linked to modern man's alteration of natural habitats, as some propose, but instead likely evolved as an adaptation for winter survival in northern regions, through trial and error, centuries ago.

HISTORIC MIGRATIONS

Famous photographer and naturalist George Shiras III contended that during the early 1800s, before major logging of the mature pine forests, whitetails living along the south shore of Lake Superior in Upper Michigan migrated 75 miles or more to their favored wintering grounds in northern Wisconsin.

According to Shiras, "Doubtless the great depth of snow in this region was the original cause of the fall migration of deer, and the habit had finally become so fixed by inheritance that long before there was any apparent necessity, the retirement took place. The deer traveled southward on many trails, which by centuries of use had become about two feet broad, clear of obstructions, and deeply cut in banks and soft ground. In swamps they were like the caribou trails found in Newfoundland.

"The fall migration was always in the form of a drift before cold northwesterly wind. Whenever if in the progress of the migrations such a wind ceased or veered so as to blow from the southward, the deer at once stopped traveling. This phenomenon was so well known among hunters that they promptly abandoned the hunt as soon as the favoring wind ceased."

Today, many wildlife managers discredit claims of such lengthy, massive whitetail migrations. However, historical notes from the region indicate that Indians frequently employed "drift fencing" to assist them in killing large numbers of whitetails during certain times of the year. As late as 1850, J. W. Foster and J. D. Whitney, while reporting on Upper Michigan geology, noted the following: "Within this township [Iron County] the Mackigamig [River] receives from the right its two principal tributaries, the Mitchikau or Fence River and the Nebegomiwini or Night-watching River. The origin of these terms as explained by our voyageurs was this: At one time the deer were observed to be very numerous about the mouth of the former, and the Indians, to secure them, built a fence from one stream to the other. They [deer] would follow rather than leap this barrier, until they were entrapped by their concealed foe. This method of capturing the deer is also practiced on the Menominee." A similar report from northeastern Wisconsin [Vilas County] claimed that three Indians employing a 15-mile-long fence killed 150 deer "for their hides only" in a few days.

If Indians were indeed that successful in capturing deer with fencing, deer must have been either

In western plains states, whitetails may winter in brushy draws, marshy basins or other areas of sparse vegetation, provided a readily available food source is located within a short distance of the protective cover.

fantastically abundant locally or, more likely, moved through the area in great numbers at certain intervals, probably during early winter and spring. Otherwise, such laborious fence-building projects would hardly have been worthwhile, as the Indian had little spare time to fritter away on ventures that did not produce.

There are also early reports from Wisconsin indicating that deer in northern parts of the state sometimes migrated southward in winter. In the 1840s, T. J. Cram stated that the Indians of the Lac Vieux Desert vicinity moved southward, "following the deer for the winter hunt." And when Richard Dart came to Green Lake County in 1840, he observed that "deer were plentiful, except when they went south in winter to escape the cold."

YARDING BEHAVIOR

Today, deer in northern Wisconsin and Upper Michigan travel in all directions from where they live in

summer to reach their favored wintering grounds, but the vast majority of them leave areas of deep snow cover and travel southward to spend the winter in areas that receive less snowfall. And although most deer in this region travel less than 10 miles to reach protective cover in winter, some of those living in central Upper Michigan travel over 50 miles.

A host of factors interact to influence the migratory distance of northern whitetails. Generally speaking, however, those living where the topography is relatively flat tend to travel somewhat farther than those that occupy hilly country where cover types are more interspersed. Even in Michigan's Upper Peninsula, for example, studies have revealed that deer living in the eastern half of the peninsula, where the terrain is gently rolling, travel significantly farther, on average, to reach their winter yards than do those living in the peninsula's rugged and hilly western half (9.3 versus 7.5 miles, respectively).

The majority of winter migrations in the northern portions of whitetail range take deer to areas experiencing less snowfall than occurs on the herds' summer ranges.

Concentrations of deer on winter yards present a "bottleneck" of population control in regions with high summer deer densities. If winter habitat can't support the crowded winter populations, many deer may starve before spring arrives.

Heavily browsed red cedar indicates a yarding area exceeding its winter carrying capacity. As the browse line increases in height, smaller deer and fawns will be unable to reach the tree limbs.

Adult bucks tend to travel somewhat farther than does and fawns to reach wintering areas. Bucks younger than two years old, in particular, sometimes exhibit unusually long movements between their summer and winter ranges. In central Minnesota, unusually lengthy movements, such as a 165-mile trek made by a yearling buck, are sometimes thought to be made by dispersers establishing new ranges. However, one adult doe traveled 85 miles, suggesting that some deer may routinely travel exceptionally long distances in certain open habitat.

Most, but not all, whitetails become quite sedentary during midwinter. In eastern South Dakota, though, Rollin Sparrowe and Paul Springer reported that "a herd of 48-80 animals used a 50-acre marsh, feeding on waste corn and browsing on willow and aspen in the marsh. This herd commonly ranged over parts of six adjoining sections (square miles), including two miles of river bottom." This was apparently one of those cases where the high-energy [corn] diet allowed deer to be unusually active and utilize sparse cover for shelter.

In northern forested areas, the amount of area traveled by deer during winter is quite variable and tends to decrease with the increasing severity of winter. Rongstad and Lewis found northern Wisconsin deer cover an average of 455 to 750 acres during the winter period, quite similar to that for deer in central Minnesota, but considerably greater than the 334 acres reported for deer in the Adirondacks of New York. Some of the smallest winter ranges—109 acres for females— were reported by Nelson and Mech for deer living in northern Minnesota.

Deer yard size tends to vary with winter severity. Generally, smaller areas of shelter, possibly only 50 to 100 acres in size, may suffice where snowfall is light, but larger areas of protective conifer cover are needed by deer wintering in heavy snow country. But not all portions of large conifer swamp deer yards are used by deer every winter. For example, Upper Michigan's Petrel Grade Deer Yard is part of a 40-square-mile conifer swamp area—referred to as the Cusino Deer Yard Complex— where deer are sometimes restricted to about two square miles during periods of especially deep snow.

Certain large deer yarding areas are critically important to deer occupying vast areas of summer range. For example, the 360-square-mile Mead Deer Yard located in central Upper Michigan serves as wintering cover for deer that occupy summer ranges scattered over a 1,400-square-mile area. An estimated 43,000 whitetails used this yard in 1987, but about 11,000 had died there during the winter of 1985-86. (Corporate forest-management practices emphasizing the production of wood products, as advocated by the primary landowner, have become highly controversial. Corporate operations have led to the fragmentation and degradation of hemlock and white cedar stands that provide valuable thermal cover for whitetails in winter.)

Northern white cedar, the lightest in weight of any commercial wood in the United States, is an excellent winter browse for whitetails. When growing in dense, fairly mature stands, it provides deer with extremely effective thermal shelter from harsh weather. This species of cedar grows primarily in southeastern Canada, the Upper Great Lakes region, and eastward into Maine and Nova Scotia. It occupies about 2 million acres in the northern Lakes States, and more than half of that amount occurs in Michigan.

White cedar can be found growing in both pure and mixed stands, mostly in swamps, but also on uplands. Trees commonly associated in swamps with white cedar are balsam fir, spruce (black, white, and red), tamarack, black ash, and red maple. On the better drained upland soils, yellow and paper birch, quaking aspen, eastern hemlock, eastern white pine, and American elm commonly grow in white-cedar-dominated stands. The pure white cedar stand will usually perpetuate itself, whereas the associated species tend to gradually replace it in mixed stands after cutting or other disturbance.

Analysis of microclimates within conifer swamp deer yards reveals that wide differences exist among various units of the yard. No single niche provides deer with maximum protection from cold, windy weather and deep snow cover and also provides adequate food supplies. For that reason, a conifer swamp's location relative to other forest or farmland types that might provide a source of food, as well as the size and configuration of the swamp's protective cover, becomes critically important in determining a given swamp area's value as wintering cover for deer.

Generally, average temperatures differ by only a few degrees among niches of a deer yard, but the amount of wind, resultant air chill (convective heat loss), and snow accumulations vary tremendously. Compared to dense stands of 60- to 80-year-old white cedar, wind flows average from five to 30 times greater in sapling-sized white cedar or mixed hardwoods and conifers, and 60 to 200 times greater in the adjacent uplands. Also, as would be expected, the closed canopy of mature cedars is more efficient in snow interception and storage, which appreciably reduces the amount of snow collecting on the forest floor. Snow that does sift through the thick overstory also tends to pack more firmly, greatly improving travel conditions, as compared to those thick, fluffy snows that accumulate in open habitats.

An ideal yarding area would provide whitetails with adequate food, protection from predators, shelter from wind and snow, and overhead cover that retains thermal energy. Unfortunately, very few deer yards exhibit all these features.

Within the cedar swamp itself, snow conditions may vary appreciably, depending upon the total annual snowfall, temperature, relative humidity, wind action, and amount of sunlight. These factors and the compaction of snow through partial melting and refreezing sometimes create a strong base and excellent support for deer. When I studied snow support quality among niches of the Petrel Grade Deer Yard, located in Alger County of Upper Michigan, differences were slight during a severe winter, averaging about ten percent better in the densely stocked mature cedars. The following year, however, which was comparatively mild, midwinter snow support values in the mature cedar stand averaged 22 to 44 percent better than in younger cedar stands or in mixed hardwood-conifers. The poorest support values were always found in sapling-sized cedars — the best browse niche within the yard — where surface crusts were commonly weakened by full sunshine and comparatively high midday temperatures. This condition, plus the presence of air pockets in the hummocky snowpack, resulted in particularly hazardous travel conditions for deer among the young cedars.

When compared to the other cover types, the mature conifer swamp cover exhibits the narrowest temperature ranges, offering good protection from sharply dropping temperatures, in particular, and the warmest average temperatures during the coldest weather. However, average temperatures are generally higher in the adjacent upland during late winter. That is, the swamp apparently cools down more slowly than the uplands early in the winter, but it also warms up more slowly towards spring, with only a slight difference in average temperatures during the interim.

Certainly, none of the environments I sampled offered deer a more comfortable microclimate or better travel conditions during the coldest months than the dense stand of mature cedars. A notable disadvantage of such cover, of course, is that very little browse grows in the heavily shaded understory. And snow not only accumulates more slowly in the heavy swamp cover, it also melts at a much slower rate. In spring, a foot of snow may remain in the dense conifers when the uplands are already snow-free.

Deer movements within individual yards will be influenced primarily by the arrangement of forest stands supplying food and shelter. Travel between the various cover types offering either food or shelter is usually on trails, even during times with minimal snow cover. The same travel paths may be used each winter and are sometimes followed on a year-round basis. Trails generally follow the path of least resistance, and deer quickly re-establish them after fresh snowfall.

Trails in fields outside a deer yard indicate the animals are feeding on jackpine, a species of relatively low nutritive value—and an indication that browse within the yard itself is seriously depleted.

Once snow depths inhibit travel even within the deer yard, whitetails will restrict their movements to heavily used trails to find food.

Although deer may wander about to forage, traveling from shrub to shrub, such widespread foraging diminishes once snow conditions are such that deer sink from 18 to 24 inches into the snow. Once deer sink more than 30 inches, there is very little movement off trails, and well-packed trails used while feeding will connect with those used mainly for travel, forming an elaborate system of interconnecting trails. In some areas, a person can walk for a mile or more by following these interconnected pathways. But individual deer probably travel less than half that distance when traveling from favored bedding sites to feed, the distance being dependent not only upon weather and snow factors but also upon the quantity and quality of food at the end of those trails.

In the Adirondacks, William Severinghaus observed that heavily used deer trails generally warned of impending malnutrition among yarded whitetails. According to Severinghaus, "When individual deer tracks outnumber deer trails and group tracks, deer are foraging enough to maintain their physical condition. Conversely, when deer trails and group tracks equal or outnumber individual deer tracks, their foraging range has become so restricted that they are unable to secure adequate nourishment."

The primary methods by which heat is lost from a

deer's body include radiation, convection, conduction, and evaporation. Of these, radiation and convective losses are normally of greatest importance and are the primary factors governing the deer's need for shelter and determining prime deer bedding sites during especially cold and windy weather.

Recall, however, that a deer's diet will also have considerable influence upon its need for shelter. The amount of digestible energy in the diet, in particular, can be an important factor determining where a deer will or won't bed. For example, Aaron Moen found that deer in western Minnesota readily bedded in open fields, despite brisk northwest winds accompanied by day and night temperatures that hovered between 0 and -34 degrees Fahrenheit for an entire week, as long as they had ready access to a high-energy diet of corn and soybeans.

Even in the absence of appreciable snow cover, however, browse-nourished deer tend to retreat to shelter among dense conifers when temperatures drop below 10 degrees Fahrenheit or when the combination of cold and strong winds cause excessive air chill. As a rule, deer are usually less active, and remain bedded longer, during periods of high winds and low temperatures and during heavy snowfall. They've been reported to remain in their beds 36 hours or more during blizzards.

A problem with deer yards that provide dense conifer cover is that little sunlight reaches the forest floor and, as a result, little or no vegetation grows close to the ground where deer can readily find browse.

During severe weather, deer beds tend to be concentrated in the yard core area, or "yard nucleus," where shelter is more important than food, as compared to the "yard periphery," where there is less shelter but more food. Based on studies conducted in Maine, when snow is 20 inches or deeper, most deer beds are used repeatedly, and most fresh beds (generally spaced about five to 15 feet apart) occur in groups of three or more. There is definite safety in numbers when deer are subjected to harsh winter conditions and potential threat from predators. Regardless of the environment, though, peak social group size among whitetails is generally found during January and February. Certainly the alertness of a number of deer, especially when some are winter-experienced, adds to the survival prospects of associated young animals experiencing their first winter season. Multiple deer also do a better job of maintaining packed trails, which are critical to the whitetail's mobility and escape from predators.

In winter, optimal group size seems to be around five or six deer per group, but sometimes dozens of deer may travel and feed together and bed in close proximity. The most stable social groups will normally consist of related does and their fawns, with several such groups sometimes coming together to form larger groups. But even unrelated does without close kin seem compelled to seek compatible associates when stressed by cold weather and heavy snow cover. A large aggregation of deer will also create a system of trails that can serve as escape routes when deer are chased by predators. Also, socially compatible deer that bed in groups provide greater sensory capability for detecting predators, which permits each deer to spend less time alert and more time feeding and ruminating. An aggregation's quail-like scattering when confronted with danger also tends to confuse predators. Despite their grouping habit, however, there is no evidence of deer huddling to conserve body heat.

When stressed by cold weather and an inadequate diet, deer tend to select bed sites carefully to conserve body heat. When bedded, a deer tucks its legs underneath its body, thereby reducing the amount of conductive heat loss from the lower, more thinly haired portions of their legs. In 20 inches of soft snow, a bedded deer will sink about ten inches. As a result, it exposes less of its body to the adverse effects of convective heat loss. Careful analysis of deer beds also reveals that deer tend to select bedding sites beneath the crowns of sizable conifers, which greatly reduces the radiant loss of body heat during cold clear nights. When severely stressed, the bedded deer will curl its head to its side—the position commonly adopted by starving whitetails—thereby reducing its total body surface exposed to convective and radiant heat loss.

Adult bucks prefer to frequent the peripheral areas of deer yards, away from does and fawns, and often bed on ridges overlooking swamp edges where they can easily detect predators.

Not surprisingly, then, favored deer bedding sites change from day to night with variations in weather severity as the winter progresses and as deer deplete their fat stores. During warm sunny days, especially as are likely to occur during late winter, deer will more likely bed in sunlit openings within conifer cover or on open south slopes on the uplands adjacent to dense conifers. Here they benefit from solar radiation and good visibility, allowing them to quickly retreat to the protective swamp conifers if suddenly threatened by roaming predators or man.

When compared to well-fattened does and fawns, mature bucks, usually lean after the rut, should be at a decided disadvantage during winter. Nonetheless, the buck's larger body size may compensate somewhat for his lack of fat stores when faced with cold weather and deep snow. Not only do bucks have longer legs, enabling them to plow through greater snow depths, but the larger-bodied bucks retain body heat much more efficiently (Bergmann's Rule), meaning they can probably make do with poorer-quality shelter in order to occupy habitat that has better food sources.

Although rather poorly documented, there is fair evidence that mature whitetail bucks sometimes segregate from does and fawns even during the winter season. Winter segregation of the sexes has been reported in mule and black-tailed deer, elk, red deer, bighorn sheep, and other ungulates. In Texas, for example, where deer are not subjected to harsh winter weather and do not exhibit seasonal shifts in range occupation, whitetail bucks commonly regroup and segregate from does and fawns after the rut.

Sex segregation among whitetails is considerably more difficult to identify on northern range once bucks cast their antlers and migrate to dense conifer cover. But even then, various investigators have reported that mature bucks are more likely to settle in peripheral areas of wintering cover, probably where browse is of better quality or more abundant, whereas does and fawns are more likely to seek core areas of the yard that provide superior shelter. My own observations indicate that adult bucks prefer to regroup after the rut and segregate from does and fawns during winter, even if it requires longer travel to reach a common food source. They are also more likely to favor bedding sites with good visibility. Bucks I've studied normally sought daytime beds away from groups of does and fawns, and seemed to prefer bedding in groups of two or three, often beneath large hemlocks on ridges along swamp edges. There they have good visibility and can easily detect approaching predators.

Based upon measurements of deer activity in the Petrel Grade Deer Yard during the 1960s, I concluded

Studies indicate that after the rut adult bucks resume their fraternal groupings and often winter together in traditional areas along with young bucks dispersing from maternal clans.

Not only do whitetails become much less active during midwinter, but weakened deer also change their daily (circadian) activity rhythm as winter progresses. During early winter, when deer are still normally in good physical condition, they exhibit a daily rhythm with five prominent peaks of activity spaced from four to six hours apart. They move about and feed most heavily around sunrise, midday, sunset, and twice during the night, a pattern that well-nourished deer hold throughout winter and probably exhibit throughout all seasons. By midwinter, however, malnourished does and fawns become most active during the warmest part of the day (from mid-morning until sunset) and greatly decrease their nighttime travel, an energy-conserving adjustment that undoubtedly serves to reduce body heat-loss.

Although much will depend upon the richness and availability of food sources and deer physical condition, the acreage that deer use within a yarding complex tends to decrease as winter weather severity increases, becoming more and more limited to sites of prime shelter as snow depths build and travel conditions become hazardous. Even mature bucks may be forced to abandon their preferred peripheral yarding cover and retreat to core areas of the yard if conditions become severe enough. But it is generally the depth and supporting character of the snowpack that governs deer

that whitetails decreased their movement activity by at least 50 percent from early to midwinter, depending somewhat upon travel conditions. Periodic thawing and refreezing of the snow cover sometimes created good support conditions for deer, which stimulated travel by extremely malnourished deer and allowed them to range more freely for browse. But I found that even browse-nourished captive deer exhibited a comparable reduction in their level of activity during midwinter, suggesting that certain entrained rhythms, probably cued to changes in photoperiod, were involved.

Early in winter, prior to heavy snowfall, whitetails' daily activity peaks resemble those exhibited during summer. By midwinter, however, their movement activities will decrease by at least 50 percent.

mobility and area use; plowing through deep snow requires energy, and increases risk from predation, which may or may not be offset by the amount of energy gained in foods eaten.

Throughout the deep snow country of the Upper Great Lakes and the Northeast, snow depths of two to three feet during midwinter are common, and accumulations of four to five feet are not unusual in those areas that annually receive from 200 to 300 inches of snow. However, to wintering whitetails, even more important than total snow depth is the composition of the snowpack and the depth to which deer sink into the snow.

The first major snow accumulations generally consist of light fluffy snow particles of low density. Deer in good physical condition can readily wade through such accumulations with minimal effort. Periodic thaws, sifting action of wind, and added weight of new snow generally causes the mass to settle and laminate by midwinter. Depending upon many different factors, the compacted snow sometimes creates difficult travel for deer. Nevertheless, under the right conditions, snow sometimes becomes so dense, and the surface crusts so hard, that deer can literally walk on top of the snow. As a result, the deer not only enjoy unrestricted travel, they also then have the ability to reach much higher for browse.

Deer running or bounding on snow will exert many

times the pressure of standing or walking animals, of course, and more easily penetrate hard-crusted snow when in flight. And although deer may wander somewhat farther away from protective cover on hard snow cover, they still seem to sense their potential vulnerability. Seldom do they travel long distances away from winter cover, and only rarely do they return to their summer range as long as deep snow cover persists during the midwinter period.

Depending upon prevailing temperatures, snow depths, and the rate of snowmelt, deer sometimes

When a snow becomes crusted, it may support deer walking on the surface. When they encounter predators and are required to run, however, whitetails' small, sharp hooves will penetrate the thin, treacherous crust.

experience extremely hazardous and exhausting travel conditions when weather begins to warm up during spring break-up. Since deer are then in poorest condition, they must confine their movements to hard-packed trails to avoid sinking through the softened snow base. But it is also during this time of the year that hard surface crusts form when a thawing day is followed by a cold night, creating brief periods of easy travel for deer.

At break-up, the supporting quality of snow deteriorates rapidly in the uplands and in sparse swamp stands as surface crusts soften and the snowpack begins to rot from beneath. Snow maintains its strength considerably longer beneath thick conifers, where midday temperatures are lower and the rate of melt is much slower. Openings adjoining a yard tend to lose snow fastest, generally two to three weeks sooner than swamp cover, and therefore are the first places deer head for when the release period approaches.

Depending upon weather patterns, aggregations of deer, sometimes numbering in the hundreds, may mingle in open areas adjacent to yarding cover for a week or more in spring before splintering off into smaller groups and commencing their migration to distant summer ranges. But spells of cold weather during this staging period will generally cause deer to retreat temporarily to the protection of conifer cover.

SPRING MIGRATION

At winter's end, deer seem anxious to leave their wintering habitat, and most do so just as soon as the uplands become snow-free. In northern Minnesota, Nelson and Mech observed that spring migration onset always occurred after maximum daily temperature shifted from below freezing to consistently above freezing. Depending upon the rate and timing of snowmelt, spring migrations of deer in the Upper Great Lakes region and in the Northeast may commence in early March, but sometimes may be delayed until May.

For unknown reasons, some deer may linger in the wintering area long after snowmelt. During their investigations in northern Minnesota, Nelson and Mech reported that five of their study animals migrated from 11 to 23 days after snowmelt, and five others from five to seven days after snowmelt. Three of their deer migrated in late May, long after snow left, and one of them migrated late for three consecutive years. They also noted that some deer were particularly responsive to temperature changes in spring. One deer already on its summer range returned to its winter range when the temperature dropped temporarily; two others stopped or returned to winter range when temperatures decreased during migration.

Most deer commence leaving winter yards when daily temperatures begin to average above freezing. Once the spring thaw begins, whitetails vacate winter yards and return to their summer ranges.

Given such variable response to spring temperatures, Nelson and Mech propose that temperature-triggered migration may operate through increasing the deer's metabolism. That is, as these researchers theorize: "Deer that migrate early may have lower thresholds for that increase; those migrating later could have higher thresholds."

It's rather obvious that young deer are dependent upon older animals for guidance in fall when migrating long distances to reach winter yarding areas. But observations by Nelson and Mech in northern Minnesota suggest that fawns also require guidance in spring. In their study, Nelson and Mech determined that two fawns orphaned on winter range left their wintering area at break-up, but they wandered rather aimlessly during the spring and summer period, apparently because they failed to achieve close social bonds with adult female relatives. Another orphaned doe fawn left the deer yard in mid-March, but by mid-June it was back in the wintering area, having traveled a minimum of 90 miles during the interim. Therefore, when long migration distances are involved, and before their migration and summer home range traditions are fully established, fawns apparently must also be led back to their ancestral summering grounds in spring.

Duration of migration by deer to their summer range in spring tends to be more direct and faster than fall migration to wintering cover, but it still may vary from only a few hours to as much as two weeks. In central Minnesota, Rongstad and Tester found that spring migrating deer commenced traveling at any time of the day or night. They calculated that deer moved at the rate of one-half to one mile per hour while traveling from winter to summer range.

While some deer may travel non-stop to their established summering grounds, others may linger for several days in favorable habitat along the migratory route. Given that many deer travel northward in spring, or at least to summer range located in regions of heavier snowfall, such lingering is not unexpected. Generally, more prolonged migratory trips tend to occur when deer leave the wintering area early in spring and when long travel distances are involved. Nonetheless, not all migratory deer can afford to dawdle while en route to their ancestral summering grounds, as the fawning season will commence in earnest by mid-May.

WHITETAIL PREDATORS

White-tailed deer are preyed upon by a variety of predators, and, especially in winter, deer's scavenged remains serve as an important food source for many species of meat-eating birds and mammals. Today, excluding man, only the domestic dog, bobcat, coyote, mountain lion, and gray wolf can be considered effective predators of wintering whitetails.

During any given day, a deer may fail to obtain its fill of browse, but, in the long run, such a shortcoming may have minimal influence on the individual's lifetime fitness. Few failings, however, are as unforgiving—or as abruptly terminal—as a deer's failure to avoid a predator. Logically, then, predation has been a strong selective force in the evolution of the whitetail's behavioral traits during the hazardous winter season. The gray wolf, the mountain lion, and the American Indian have probably exerted the greatest

The bobcat is only one of a handful of predators whitetails encounter in the wild. Although not a primary predator of deer-sized animals, the diminutive bobcat is capable of bringing down full-grown whitetails.

selective pressure on whitetails. Together, they are largely responsible for the defensive behaviors we see whitetails exhibit through the year.

The importance of predation in the whitetail's evolutionary time is rather obvious. But there is a growing body of evidence suggesting that whitetails may also have the ability to assess and behaviorally influence their risk of being preyed upon in ecological time (during their lifetime). Steven Lima and Lawrence Dill present a rather thought-provoking discussion on this subject and argue: "While predation pressure may vary little over evolutionary time, during ecological time the risk of being preyed upon may vary greatly on a seasonal, daily, or even minute-by-minute basis. Since an animal must accomplish more in its lifetime than simply avoiding predators, its antipredator adaptations should somehow be sensitive to the current level of predation risk."

How such theory relates to decision making by white-

tails is unknown, but deer may be able to assess the risk of predation in their environment and, as a result, weigh the costs and benefits associated with various behavioral options. For example, patches of habitat may vary not only in terms of their foraging profitability but also in terms of predation risk. When the best winter food areas are also the most dangerous—as they usually are—the whitetail must trade off energy gain against the risk of predation in deciding where and when to feed. The decision to range out and feed or to stay put and not feed, then, becomes an important part of a deer's antipredator behavior; the final decision, and the outcome, may hinge upon a multitude of factors that change in importance from one area to the next and over time.

Cold temperatures and snow cover contribute significantly to the whitetail's vulnerability to predators on northern parts of its range. In winter, when high-energy food sources are scarce, deer cleverly conserve energy by

Crows and ravens are beneficiaries of deer starvation and the skills of mammalian predators that kill whitetails. The birds, always on the lookout for an easy meal, commonly scavenge whitetail remains.

*On the northern fringes of whitetail range, the presence of a flock or crows or
ravens in winter is a good indication that the carcass of a large animal,
usually a whitetail deer, is lying a short distance away.*

In winter, whitetail bucks are more solitary than does and fawns and travel more widely to obtain food. Their habits place them at greater risk of predation, but their size and strength help offset their vulnerability.

reducing their metabolism and by remaining inactive for extended periods in protective cover. Even their inactivity can be considered an antipredator adaptation, because a moving animal normally is more susceptible to predation than one that is resting. Yet even when bedded the whitetail must remain alert to, and be ready to avoid, predators that hunt them.

The tendencies of whitetails to seek shelter and to congregate ("yard-up") during severe winter weather certainly accommodate their need to conserve energy, but also serve as predator defenses in various ways. Social factors and grouping as part of yarding behavior become important aspects of antipredator behavior because individuals in a foraging group can spend less time being vigilant and more time feeding. The trail system that congregations of deer form also provides critically important avenues for escape from predators.

There are also many important trade-offs involved in the social habits and congregating behavior of deer in winter. There must be an optimal size and composition for groups of whitetails, which could change relative to weather patterns, snow conditions, social relationships, and the availability of food and shelter resources. Under some conditions, competition among group members for food could be detrimental to the survival of the subordinates.

Keen senses of sight, hearing and smell remain whitetails' first lines of defense from predators, helping them avoid the deadly animals. When contact appears unavoidable, though, deer rely upon a swift retreat to remain alive.

Deep snow is not only a hindrance to deer seeking food, it also greatly increases their chances of becoming bogged down and killed by predators that can easily course through or over deep snow.

Increasing snow depth probably represents one of the most powerful environmental factors influencing white-tailed deer behavior and welfare on winter range. Although some people might consider such thinking anthropomorphic, I suspect that deer sense their conspicuousness against a snow-covered background. As a result, they become more wary and alter their behavior accordingly. Snow that is especially deep provides poor support for deer, increases their energy expenditure while attempting to travel through it, thus greatly restricting their ability to find adequate food and contributing to weakened animals more vulnerable to predation. Under certain conditions, deer predators, most of which weigh less than deer, also sometimes gain a decided advantage by being able to travel atop crusted snow, whereas bounding deer may break through the snow crust and flounder helplessly, making even strong, healthy deer exceedingly vulnerable to predation.

EARLY AMERICANS

Although early American Indians employed a wide variety of hunting techniques and harvested whitetails year around, certain documentation reveals Indians killed more than 60 percent of their deer during winter. And, in the North, where deep snow and cold temperatures were obstacles to often more productive drive-type hunts (sometimes using fire), the Menominee and Ojibwa Indians sometimes snared deer along heavily packed trails or used snowshoes to run deer down in deep snow.

Historically, even the early voyageurs and fur traders occasionally took advantage of crusted snow when hunting deer. As early as the winter of 1661-62, French explorer and fur trader Pierre Radisson found whitetails fairly plentiful in northwestern Wisconsin and easy prey during a period of deep and crusted snow cover. In his quaint style, he wrote: "The weather continued so 3 dayes that we needed no racketts [snowshoes] more, for the snow hardened much. The small staggs [presumably whitetails] are as if they were stakes in it after they made 7 or 8 capers. It's an easy matter for us to take them and cutt their throats with our knives."

Many old records refer to certain winters being especially hard on northern deer because of deep and crusted snow. Father Jacques Marquette spent the hard winter of 1674-75 at the present site of Chicago. On January 24 he referred to the weather being hard on all wild animals, and on March 20, the deer were so lean that many of those killed were abandoned.

In Wisconsin, the winters of 1806-07 and 1856-57 were also tough on deer, and easy on predators. According to one account, "In March 1807 a crust

Deer are not only vulnerable to carnivores such as wolves, coyotes, mountain lions, and bobcats during periods of deep snow. Historical accounts relate that white pioneers and Indians commonly ran down deer and slaughtered them in mass numbers.

formed on the snow and Indians tomahawked every deer that could be found, for sheer amusement." Similar adverse snow conditions developed in December 1856, when a crust about one-half inch thick reportedly formed over a deep snowpack. According to Jonathan Cartwright, considered an experienced hunter of his period, "This winter was the hardest on deer of any I have ever known. White men and Indians (Menominee) slaughtered them in great numbers. They would put on snowshoes, and taking a hatchet, but no gun, would strike them down ... One man told me that he killed ten in one day, and that in some places the Indians had taken them by hundreds."

Whitetails faced similar hazardous snow conditions during the winters of 1868-69 and 1887-88. Newspaper accounts from northern Wisconsin relate instances where, because of crusted snow in February, "deer were slaughtered in wholesale fashion." Ambrose Hummel of Green Bay reportedly "killed 88 deer that season along the Menominee River." In 1888, two hunters at Bryant "caught a herd of 17 deer in the deep snow and killed all of them."

Had I not experienced a comparable advantage over deer due to snow conditions, it would be quite easy for me to discredit such accounts as being exaggerations. Believe me, given the right circumstances, it's not especially difficult to run down and capture a whitetail in deep snow, provided, of course, one can stay on its track.

My first winter (1964-65) at the Cusino Wildlife Research Station was a severe one. Although total snowfall was not particularly heavy (151 inches), continued cold weather held snow depths in the two- to three-foot range for two and a half months. Despite the deep snow, we had difficulty live-trapping deer in the square-mile enclosure and, by the end of March, were concerned that we would not be able to complete our annual trap-out census. Quite by accident, however, we learned it was possible to run them down on snowshoes.

One day, a deer I had spooked almost ran into two men doing some maintenance work on a deer live-trap. At the last moment, the startled deer veered off the packed trail and promptly bogged down in deep snow. The three of us pounced on the animal, bound its legs, and hauled it back to the station for data gathering. Five of us then proceeded to track down and capture the remaining five animals, by hand, in three days.

I recall being involved in capturing three of those deer. After several hours of being chased, a small male fawn finally just stood its ground and pitifully challenged us when we grabbed it. In desperation, one

large doe actually tried to crawl into a fox den located beneath a large pine stump, in an apparent attempt to hide. As I approached along her track, I was amazed to see only her hindquarters protruding above the snow. I unbuckled my snowshoes for a quick release, then shuffled closer and kicked off the snowshoes just before grabbing the doe's hind legs. Needless to say, I had my hands full until help arrived.

The last deer to be captured, an adult doe, insisted upon racing back and forth in Hickey Creek, a shallow hard-bottomed stream that bisects the enclosure. She would run, then hide in the alders along the stream bank. Lou Verme worked one side of the stream and I the other, until we'd flush her from hiding. After several such trips along the stream, we converged where we'd last seen the doe—but she'd disappeared!

Lou and I met in mid-stream, on a dilapidated slab-covered bridge that crossed the stream with a mere one foot of clearance above the water. While standing there, pondering our next move, I happened to look down into the water just beneath my feet. There was the doe, completely submerged with only her snout, eyes, and ears visible above the water. "Lou," I sputtered, "there she is."

There's something special about making eye-contact with a deer. Somehow this doe sensed I had detected her the moment our eyes met. Within a split-second, before either Verme or I conjured up enough nerve to leap into the two feet of icy water, she bolted from the stream and headed cross-country, but we later ran her down in deep snow.

Archives abound with accounts of Indians and early pioneers occasionally killing enormous numbers of whitetails. These historical narratives rather vividly illustrate the extreme vulnerability of deer to human predation during times of deep and crusted snow. Historically, single deer—or small groups of them—that chose to remain in isolated patches of cover surrounded by deep snow must have fallen easy prey to persistent ancient Indians armed only with crude hand-held weapons. One can only surmise that wolves and mountain lions also periodically experienced ideal snow conditions that permitted them to dispatch wintering whitetails with far greater than usual success.

On the other hand, it may not have been such an easy task for the Indian, or even a wolf or mountain lion, to capture deer congregated in vast areas of dense conifer swamp cover. There the deers' elaborate trail system enhanced their prospects of escape from flint-tipped arrows or flashing fangs.

MOUNTAIN LIONS

Although now virtually absent from the eastern United States (except for isolated pockets in Florida) and most of Canada, mountain lions historically had one of the most extensive distributions of any mammal in the Western Hemisphere. The big cats originally ranged from the Atlantic to the Pacific and from Patagonia to northern British Columbia. No doubt they were formidable predators of whitetails, which probably served as their main source of food.

Now much more dependent upon mule deer as a food source, mountain lions still prey heavily upon whitetails in some western states and in southwestern Canada. In Manitoba, mountain lions have increased substantially since the 1970s, apparently because of sharply rising white-tailed deer numbers.

The mountain lion is a strong, solitary, wide-ranging hunter; an adult male may cover a home range of around 30 square miles. The lion uses its keen sense of smell and sight to locate a deer, then stalks it, creeping close before making a short charge and pouncing upon the victim's back. The fatal wounds are generally bites to the back of the deer's neck. Although quite capable of killing the largest of whitetail bucks without difficulty, given what is known about their habits of preying on mule deer in winter, mountain lions probably prey most heavily upon whitetails that are young, old, or weakened by malnutrition.

In the eastern U.S., mountain lions have virtually ceased to exist. In some western states and in mountainous regions of Canada, however, this strong, solitary predator still depends heavily on whitetail and mule deer as a mainstay in its diet.

GRAY WOLVES

Gray wolves, oftentimes called timber wolves, are also effective whitetail predators and probably played an equally prominent role in shaping white-tailed deers' behavioral adaptations for winter survival. Although human progress has largely eliminated the wolf from much of its former range, wolves and whitetails still share common range in northern Wisconsin, Michigan, Minnesota, and much of southern Canada. With continued protection and the current emphasis on biodiversity and ecological systems management, the wolf's future probably looks brighter now than it has during the past 50 years. Someday, possibly soon, the mere presence of wolves may become a key factor in determining regional deer management strategies.

Where the two species share geographic range, white-tailed deer usually constitute more than 90 percent of the wolf's winter diet. Most of these deer are secured as fresh kills. Based upon his extensive research conducted in the Superior National Forest of northeastern Minnesota, David Mech, a recognized world authority on the gray wolf, concluded that the average wolf might kill about 15 adult deer per year, provided other prey such as beaver and moose were also available. But under most conditions today, he proposes, "Wolves do not seem to be able to limit a deer population seriously. But in some circumstances they can actually exterminate local whitetail populations."

Given the right circumstances, wolves can be potent deer killers, especially in winter, when their success is closely linked to the severity of weather and snow conditions. Investigations conducted in northeastern Minnesota, for example, revealed that wolves killed more whitetails during severe winters than they did during mild ones, but their kill rate was more directly related to snow depth than to temperature. Nelson and Mech proposed that snow depth influences deer vulnerability to predation in two ways: "First, it acts as a physical impedance to escape. Wolves have a lighter track load and they sink less in deep snow than deer. Second, restricted mobility and increased energy costs from travel in deep snow reduce deer fat reserves." Hence, toward the end of a tough winter, wolves can capture deer more readily in deep snow, especially when the prey are fat-depleted and weakened from malnutrition.

Mech suggests that deep snow also hinders wolves "often more so than deer, because wolves run at a shallower angle and thus meet more resistance than do deer, which tend to spring up out of the snow. On the other hand, wolves gain about twice as much support from snow as do deer. Sometimes in the early winter or

Where their ranges overlap, gray wolves rely predominantly on white-tailed deer as a food source. In the majority of instances where their populations intermingle, however, wolves do not seriously limit deer populations.

Wolf predation on deer peaks during long, severe winters when whitetails are particularly weakened by poor nutrition and loss of body reserves due to prolonged exposure to cold.

late spring a crust develops that is thick enough to support wolves but too thin to support deer, and this gives the former a temporary advantage."

In Minnesota, wolves killed a disproportionate number of fawns in poor physical condition and adult deer five or more years of age, whereas yearlings and middle-aged deer were less vulnerable to wolf predation. The Minnesota wolves also killed proportionately more adult bucks than adult does, findings that mimicked the results of earlier investigations conducted by Douglas Pimlott and his co-workers in Algonquin Provincial Park in Ontario.

Based upon their examination of 676 dead deer that had been killed by wolves during the period 1958 to 1965, the Canadian investigators concluded that deer were the sole prey of wolves for considerable periods during the winter. These researchers also observed that wolves more completely utilized the deer they killed during mild winters, when deer were tough to catch, as compared to severe winters when deer were more vulnerable (82 versus 44 percent completely consumed, respectively). Contrary to other reports, however, the Canadian studies revealed no evidence that wolves killed deer purely for "sport," regardless of deer vulnerability.

Nelson and Mech found deer to be at greater risk and most vulnerable to wolf predation while migrating from summer to winter range during the fall period. Despite the relatively short migration periods, the biologists estimated that daily predation rates on fall-migrating whitetails were 16 to 107 times those of yarded deer. In addition, Nelson's and Mech's data showed at least a ninefold greater mortality rate due to wolf predation for nonyarded versus yarded deer, which exemplifies the adaptive value of whitetail yarding behavior. It's interesting to note, however, that during mid-winter, nonyarding adult males suffered lower wolf predation rates than nonyarding adult females, suggesting that the greater size and strength of bucks may provide some advantage outside of deer yards or in peripheral yard habitat.

Because fall migrations occur during and after breeding, the Minnesota researchers speculate that decreased wariness and declining body condition as a result of breeding may be factors that increase adult buck vulnerability to predation while en route to wintering areas. In addition, the incidence of leg arthritis is greater in older male deer, which probably decreases their ability to escape predators. The researchers, however, were unable to explain the lower incidence of wolf predation upon deer during spring migration, a period when deer should be more vulnerable due to their poor physical condition at that time of year.

Injured deer are particularly susceptible to predation. Fawns in poor condition and adult deer older than five years of age experience the highest percentage of wolf mortality.

Research indicates that rut-weakened bucks en route to wintering areas suffer a disproportionate degree of wolf mortality. Once on their winter areas, however, non-yarding bucks suffer lower wolf predation rates than do yarded deer.

According to Mech, "Watching wolves hunting deer, it is easy to see how they end up killing certain classes that probably have low survivability. Wolves are hunting whenever they travel. When they sense a deer, they try to move closer to it without spooking it. However, most deer are quite alert. As soon as they detect approaching wolves, they flee. The wolves then make a half-hearted chase or are left far behind. Most chases last only a few minutes in time and less than about 1,200 yards in distance, although a most unusual pursuit lasted more than two hours and covered at least 12.9 miles." In other words, although wolves attempt to catch any deer they can, their physical abilities normally restrict them to capturing primarily disadvantaged or debilitated animals.

Whitetails are reasonably well adapted to endure harsh winters, even under the watchful eye of the gray wolf. Notwithstanding such adaptation, according to Mech, there is good evidence "that whitetail populations in the northern part of the species' range may succumb to combinations of extreme adverse conditions, including wolf predation. Where this has been documented, a series of record-breaking severe winters combined with a high wolf density and relatively poor deer habitat proved too much for local whitetail populations. In northeastern Minnesota, for example, deer were decimated in an area of about 1,200 square

The coyote, like the white-tailed deer, is an opportunist. It has extended its range greatly over the last half millennium and is now found wherever whitetails are known to exist.

miles of their poorest habitat from 1968 to 1974."

Although wolves sometimes hunt individually, they are more often social hunters. Wolves tend to travel in packs of five to seven animals (but sometimes as large as 15 to 30), and roam over extensive winter territories from 50 to 200 square miles in size. Around each wolf pack's territory lies a "buffer zone"—a one-and-a-quarter-mile-wide strip—where wolves of neighboring packs spend little time. Wolves will kill members of neighboring packs and tend to avoid such encounters, which most likely occur in buffer zones. As a result, the area between wolf-pack territories is the least hunted by wolves.

While monitoring the deer decline in northeastern Minnesota, Mech observed that surviving deer were almost exclusively found along the edges of wolf packs' territories, in the buffer zones avoided by wolves. He proposed that such a relationship "…is important in helping to perpetuate the prey population, thereby also helping to perpetuate the predator and, thus, the entire predator-prey system." According to his theory, "…because wolf packs tend to avoid intensive use of buffer zones, deer inhabiting those areas tend to survive longer and form a reservoir for maintaining and recovering deer populations in the wolf territory cores."

Since adult deer are most vulnerable to wolf predation during winter, Mech's proposed theory implies that the largest, longest-lasting, and most secure deer yards would be located along wolf pack buffer zones. According to Mech, "This is currently the case in northeastern Minnesota. The theory predicts and observations confirm that some deer might concentrate in more temporary yards in [wolf-pack] territory cores, but under adverse conditions those yards are the first to disappear."

COYOTES

With the demise of the mountain lion and as the gray wolf slowly gave ground to human encroachment, the coyote has assumed a more prominent, and often highly controversial, predatory role. Restricted primarily to the open plains of western North America during per-Columbian times, the clever coyote now ranges from well into Central America to near Point Barrow, Alaska, eastward to Hudson Bay, New Brunswick, and Maine, and across most of the western and midwestern U.S. There is also evidence of a gradual extension of the coyote's range into the southeastern United States. While not nearly as effective as the wolf or mountain lion, the coyote is sometimes a potentially important predator of wintering whitetails.

The wolf and coyote have never been compatible associates. In fact, wolves probably chase and try to kill every coyote they encounter. Competition for food and

As a rule, coyotes avoid wolves, which are known killers of their smaller cousins. But coyotes are not above following wolf tracks to scavenge predated deer wolves leave in their wake.

direct killing by wolves are given as the primary factors contributing to the coyote's disappearance from Isle Royale in Lake Superior. Even today, where the two species live in the same general area, each occurs in highest densities where the other is less common.

In Manitoba, Ludwig Carbyn observed that wolves frequently killed coyotes but did not consume them. He found no evidence that coyotes avoided wolves during most of the year, but definitely did so from mid- to late winter. Carbyn theorized that differences in snow conditions, and learning on the coyote's part, may be involved in the coyote's changing response to wolves as the winter progresses. When snow is deep and soft, coyotes are hindered more than wolves. However, since coyotes often trailed wolves through deep soft snow, Carbyn theorized that although coyotes may avoid wolves after a "refractory period," they may actually trail them at a safe distance in search of food.

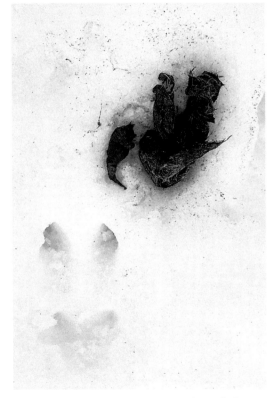

The wolf pack's buffer zone concept proposed by Mech for wolf-deer interactions appears to apply equally well, in some cases, to wolf-coyote relations. In Carbyn's study, coyotes were not always safe from wolves while in the buffer zone when wolf density was high, but overall coyote survival appeared to be greater there during years of only moderate wolf density.

Paul Paquet found coyotes scavenging wolf-killed deer within 24 hours after abandonment by wolves. Although wolves occasionally killed coyotes, Paquet saw no evidence of wolves actively searching for coyotes. In his opinion, the benefits that accrue to coyotes from feeding on carrion made available by wolves far outweighs the risks associated with being close to wolves.

Coyotes usually hunt individually or in pairs, and occasionally in packs of three to five animals. It is also noteworthy that coyotes are territorial, which limits the number of coyotes able to use a winter deer yard. This means that

Deer hair in coyote scats dropped near a whitetail track imply the deer was being trailed. While coyotes are capable of killing deer, most whitetail meals come to them in the form of carrion.

deer benefit by concentrating, leaving some coyote territories without access, or with limited access, to deer within the yarding area.

Throughout northern deer range, coyotes rely heavily upon white-tailed deer as a source of food, especially in winter. In the Upper Great Lakes Region, and in the Northeast, whitetails generally constitute half or more of the coyote's winter diet, being more important during severe winters and when other food sources, such as snowshoe hares, are scarce. Coyotes obtain most of their venison in carrion form, but some studies indicate they are quite capable of killing deer, given the right circumstances.

During the late 1950s and early 1960s, El Harger and I followed more than 800 miles of coyote tracks in the snow to determine the magnitude of coyote predation on yarded deer in northern Michigan. We compared coyote hunting success on Beaver Island, where winters tend to be relatively mild and snow depths minimal, with that in the Petrel Grade Deer Yard, a deep snow area extremely tough on deer. We found deer carrion to be the coyote's primary winter food in both areas, but deer deaths from malnutrition and coyote predation were more common in the deep snow country.

On Beaver Island, deer killed but not retrieved by

Coyote-inflicted wounds on whitetails are not uncommon, but few adult deer, especially relatively strong bucks attacked early in the season, prior to weakening by winter stress, are actually killed by coyotes.

human hunters during the fall hunting season provided coyotes their main source of food. Even the entrails discarded from legal kills and scraps of venison scattered widely about the carcasses by scavengers were dug from as much as 20 inches of snow and fed upon by coyotes. Nonetheless, only one of 15 dead deer we found could be definitely attributed to coyote predation.

Coyotes in the Petrel Grade area were considerably more successful in capturing deer, killing three fawns and one adult doe in nine known tries. In all, eight of 37 dead deer found while trailing coyotes had been attacked and died of coyote-inflicted wounds. In addition, we found eight other deer that had been killed by coyotes other than those we were following. Of the 16 coyote-killed deer examined, three were adults and 13 were fawns. All but three were killed in March and April, when deer are normally in their poorest physical condition; only three victims had appreciable fat.

Given their opportunistic nature, it is not surprising that coyotes demonstrate prey switching during winter, generally associated with changes in prey availability or vulnerability. Snowshoe hares and other small mammals are normally important early winter food items for coyotes, but deer become more important during late winter, especially during severe winters with deep crusted snow. Nearly every study conducted on northern deer range has revealed that, during early winter, coyotes feed heavily upon the carcasses of deer left from the autumn hunting seasons. Coyotes then switch to scavenging the carcasses of starved deer and kill malnourished and weakened deer when the opportunity arises during late winter.

Most studies indicate that coyotes come upon deer quite by chance, with minimal stalking, and then give chase when the surprised prey flee. In the dense conifer swamp cover characteristic of good deer yards, the coyote's chase, successful or not, usually

Coyotes tend to be solitary hunters but will also gather in groups of three to five animals to attack prey. Nonetheless, the coyote's hunting tactics, whether alone or in groups, lack the relatively sophisticated methodology demonstrated by wolves.

consists only of a short "testing" dash toward the deer. Such attempts normally only cover a couple hundred feet. As a result, coyotes more commonly bring down the smallest and weakest animals—those least likely to survive the winter.

I observed two unusually long, fruitless pursuits of deer made by single coyotes, covering 2.7 and 2.9 miles, in upland hardwood cover. In at least one of those instances, tufts of deer hair near the original point of contact suggested that the coyote had hold of the deer, at least briefly, early in the attack, probably encouraging the coyote and contributing to a longer-than-normal chase.

Coyotes tend to bring down deer from the side or rear. Although coyotes sometimes hamstring deer by biting at the hind legs, I've observed cases where the attacking coyote grabbed running deer by the neck, from the side, and brought them down with force. Under such circumstances, coyotes sometimes dispatch small deer by biting their head or upper neck, but other reports suggest that the deer die while being eviscerated. I've come upon coyotes feeding on live deer that were in the final throes of death from starvation. In such cases the coyotes merely happened along, finding the deer when it was already down and unable to rise, and commenced feeding without even attempting to kill the prey.

At least one study, conducted by Parker and Maxwell

in New Brunswick, indicated that coyotes do not restrict predation to malnourished deer. According to these biologists' findings, once deep snow cover becomes crusted, allowing coyotes to run on top but still hindering deer travel, coyotes readily attack any deer they encounter. In Parker's and Maxwell's investigation, predation on deer then resulted from chance encounters where deer were severely disadvantaged by snow conditions, and attacks were judged to be "spontaneous responses to visual stimuli." Because coyote-killed deer they examined were considered to be in excellent physical condition, Parker and Maxwell concluded: "Our data do not support the hypothesis that coyote predation on deer is insignificant and that those deer succumbing to predation would likely have died from other mortality factors... The high incidence of fawns in the sample suggests that size and behavior (slower reactions) of prey may also elicit an attack response."

The work conducted by Craig Huegel in northern Wisconsin revealed that a coyote's age and experience also play an important role in its ability to kill whitetails. In Huegel's study, juvenile coyotes failed to kill whitetails during winter, but instead scavenged other coyote kills and the remains of deer left from the hunting season. On the other hand, an adult male coyote switched from scavenging to feeding exclusively upon fresh deer kills it and other coyotes made during late winter.

Research conducted by Messier and Barrette rather convincingly showed that wintering whitetails reduce their vulnerability to coyote predation by congregating in traditional deer yards. These investigators found that pairs and packs of coyotes preferred hunting in areas of low deer density—the yarding periphery—and made the majority of deer-kills (17 of 18 known cases) there, despite a lower rate of deer encounters. In contrast, solitary coyotes showed no significant foraging tendency relative to deer density and had a more diversified winter diet, consisting primarily of scavenged deer carcasses and snowshoe hares.

From their tracking studies, Messier and Barrette concluded that "... deer killing [by coyotes] depends primarily on the opportunity to corner the quarry in deep snow where the animal is harassed until exhausted or suffocated by a throat grip. Deer must rely on a quick escape, and we believe that the density of the runways constitutes a critical element of a successful escape... In areas of low deer density, deer are therefore relatively further away from an escape route. Indeed, kill distribution indicated that a deer experiences a higher chance of being killed in these [peripheral] areas."

In winter, coyote predation on whitetails is not

limited to regions of heavy snow cover. Wherever whitetails and coyotes coexist, coyotes readily kill deer that are diseased, injured, or malnourished, and scavenge the remains of others. In Texas, for example, the importance of deer in the coyote's winter diet tends to increase when adult deer become malnourished because of drought, which decreases the amount and quality of plant forage. Also, under such conditions, coyotes more readily kill adult bucks that are physically weakened and vulnerable following the strenuous rut period.

BOBCATS

Generally, bobcats are more inclined to hunt rabbits, snowshoe hares, and other small mammals and birds, and are not usually considered a serious predator of white-tailed deer. But large bobcats are cunning, strong, and quite capable of downing healthy adult deer. Unlike coyotes, which prey heavily upon fawns, some studies have shown a preponderance

of adult deer in the bobcat's winter diet. While studying bobcat behavior in Massachusetts, Chet McCord concluded that a high occurrence of deer in the winter diet of bobcats was the result of predation and not scavenging on carrion deer carcasses.

The bobcat tends to be a nocturnal hunter. It has keen senses of vision and hearing, both of which it uses in hunting, but it is not noted for its sense of smell. The bobcat is a good climber and sometimes hunts from ambush by waiting patiently, in typical cat fashion, along well used deer trails. It may also follow deer trails until a deer is sighted or heard, then silently sneak to within pouncing distance.

According to McCord, bobcats actively hunt deer in whitetail bedding areas, but they will also attempt to catch deer in any opportune situation. He described the hunting technique employed by a bobcat as follows: "On 3 January 1971, I was following an old female bobcat

While bobcats consume relatively little deer meat in their winter diet, evidence suggests that the whitetails they do eat are killed by them rather than consumed as carrion.

Neck wounds on deer are not conclusive of an attack by any single species of predator. Mountain lions, gray wolves, coyotes, bobcats or domestic dogs will all attempt to drag down deer by employing a throat-hold.

along the edge of a pine plantation when she came to a hardwood opening and stopped. She apparently had seen a deer bedded on the opposite edge of the opening. She retraced her steps and circled, approaching the deer in the pine plantation, but from the other side. There was little ground cover, though she used every bit available in stalking within 2.6 meters (8.5 feet) of the bedded animal. In one jump the cat was on the deer, as was apparent from the struggle marks and deer hair in the snow. The deer gained its feet and escaped with the cat pursuing only four jumps."

Once a bobcat kills a deer, it will feed heavily and may remain in the vicinity of the kill for three or four days, alternately feeding and resting. As in the case of mountain lions, the bobcat may cache the uneaten deer remains, covering them with debris and snow, returning periodically to feast on the leftovers.

DOMESTIC DOGS

There is considerable evidence that the most egregious four-footed predator of wintering whitetails is the domestic dog. Although deer-killing dogs are usually considered to be stray or feral, numerous house and yard pets are guilty of such action. While dogs may pose little threat to deer in the South, in the North, especially during late winter, roving dogs can play havoc with deer

In the Upper Midwest, the greatest predator of white-tailed deer is the domestic dog. When allowed to roam at will, dogs form packs that relentlessly chase deer and kill the animals.

concentrated in yarding areas. At that time of year, crusted snow frequently supports dogs but not deer, increasing prospects for dog-kills. More importantly, unlike most natural predators, dogs tend to chase deer for long distances and to harass them, forcing them to expend energy at a time when they often have little reserve energy to waste. Because stress from continual harassment can alter the metabolic status of deer, such disturbance alone may ultimately prove fatal to deer in poor physical condition at winter's end. The importance of such harassment to pregnant does is unknown but is potentially serious and might decrease subsequent newborn fawn survival rates.

Management of habitat for wintering whitetails remains a controversial issue. Some managers propose that habitat should be managed to promote dispersion of deer during winter, thereby reducing browsing competition and providing more available browse per deer—a reasonable approach in regions where winters are not

normally severe. Such an approach could prove devastating, however, during unusually severe winters wherever wolves or coyotes pose a serious threat to deer hampered by deep crusted snow cover. Also, a series of mild winters can perpetuate deer occupation of widely scattered, poorly sheltered sites. While such dispersion may be viewed as a favorable alternative to large concentrations of deer within core areas of traditional deer yards, these satellite herds suffer high mortality rates, or even elimination, from the combined effects of malnutrition and predation during tough winters.

In areas of severe winter weather where deer are threatened by predation, promoting large yards with high deer densities is likely to minimize predation. Thus it may prove far more effective to maintain large blocks of protective cover where deer can rest in comfort in fairly high densities, safe from predators, and then create numerous patches of browse in close proximity, where deer might feed at low density with less feeding competition.

In the wild, little goes to waste. In the absence of crows and ravens, scavengers such as this magpie, coyotes, jays, or eagles (right), or any animal lucky enough to discover a deer carcass, may survive for days on the surfeit of meat.

NUTRITION AND MALNUTRITION

L ike other ruminants, whitetails possess a four-compartment stomach (rumen, reticulum, omasum and abomasum), meaning they can meet their energy needs from nutrients consumed in food plus those synthesized by the microbial bacteria and protozoa that live in their rumen. The fermentation process, or breakdown of food by the rumen microbes, is the main difference between ruminants and simple-stomached animals. One advantage of such a digestive system is that it allows an animal to digest cellulose and other complex carbohydrates found in browse and other fibrous foods typically consumed by deer.

The fermentation process is especially important to deer when only low-quality food is available, as is commonly the case during winter. However, as pointed out by Duane Ullrey, a prominent animal nutritionist from Michigan State

Whitetails may have considerable vegetation available for ingestion in winter, but they must consume digestible foods of high nutritive value to receive any real benefit from browsing on the plants.

University, "... deer are by no means super-ruminants—they cannot utilize some woody browse species as well as cattle can—and have difficulty surviving on highly lignified [woody] foods."

DIGESTION

According to Ullrey, "...the rate of forage digestion depends upon its cellulose content; succulent food being more rapidly broken down than fibrous material. The very slow rate at which low-quality browse passes through the digestive tract explains why deer 'starve'

Deer feeding solely on woody browse indicates quality foods are no longer available to them. Woody vegetation is difficult for deer to digest, and they will starve if restricted to a diet of this abundant but non-nutritious forage.

despite a full paunch." This means that foods difficult to digest are retained longer in the rumen-reticulum than are easily digested foods, restricting the amount of food a deer may consume. Such a limitation, if prolonged, will lead to severe malnutrition and, ultimately, death from starvation.

Robert Brown of Texas A & M University also observes that deer have a special problem with lignin. "Not only is it indigestible," he notes, "it can make other nutrients in the food less digestible by binding to them. And secondary plant compounds such as tannins and other phenolics can make both protein and cellulose less digestible."

This is another benefit of diet diversity, which normally prevents deer from ingesting too much of any one plant compound that inhibits digestion. Healthy deer tend to avoid eating excessive amounts of certain compounds that inhibit the action of rumen microbes, whereas starving deer are less likely to exercise such precautionary measures.

One advantage the whitetail has over simple-stomached animals, according to Brown, "is that its rumen microbes can actually produce protein. When a deer's diet lacks high-quality proteins, for example, the microbes can simply create them using whatever amino acids and other nitrogen are available." Whereas simple-stomached animals must consume a sufficient amount of food containing high-quality proteins, then, the ruminant only has to be concerned with the quantity of protein in its diet. The rumen microbes can compensate for deficiencies in protein quality.

Whitetails also have a great capacity to conserve nitrogen when protein intake is restricted, by increasing renal reabsorption and recycling of urea (the end product of dietary protein metabolism), thus reducing their nitrogen loss in urine.

Generally, among species of ruminants, there is a relationship between body size, stomach size, and feeding strategy. That is, unlike cattle and sheep, whitetails have a small stomach relative to their body size and require a fairly high-quality diet.

Whitetails' feeding habits are highly variable and opportunistic, but highly selective. Their diverse feeding habits change with the seasons, allowing them to choose a wide variety of foods, including grasses, sedges, fruits, nuts, forbs and mushrooms, in addition to portions of those shrubs and trees that best meet their nutritional requirements.

Since a whitetail's diet changes so dramatically with the seasons, it's also important to note that the whitetail's digestive tract can change with its diet, but gradually so. The amount of saliva produced, the lining of the rumen,

and the rumen's size, for example, change seasonally to compensate for the shift from succulent summer forage to a more-fibrous winter diet, and back again to more luscious foods with spring green-up. According to Brown, however, it takes from two to three weeks for the rumen microbes to completely adjust to a new diet.

The whitetail's digestive system is also well geared to predator defense. Recall from earlier discussion that, in winter, browsing can be risky for deer because snow conditions in the best food niches of wintering cover also tend to be the deepest and most hazardous. Being a

Whitetails, when a variety of foods are available to them, are selective feeders; they seek the most highly nutritious, palatable foods they can find, such as, in this case, hemlock.

ruminant, a deer can gather food quite rapidly and store it temporarily in its rumen. Later, while resting in the most comfortable and safest niche within its winter cover, the deer can rest, regurgitate, chew, and leisurely digest the food while remaining alert and ready to flee if a predator happens to come along.

WINTER FOOD

In general, deer do not require a protein-rich diet in winter. Instead, foods high in energy become more important to all deer subjected to cold-stress. Pregnant does require somewhat higher protein intake, as compared to the protein requirements of fawns and adult bucks, especially during late winter and spring, due to the accelerated growth rate of their fetuses during the last third of gestation. High-energy foods, on the other hand, equate to greater heat production necessary to balance heat losses and also provide for more-favorable rumen function.

In winter, where possible, whitetails will feed heavily upon rich farm crops such as corn, apples, rye grass, alfalfa, soybeans, and winter wheat. Even small amounts of such high-energy food tend to enhance rumen function and permit the animal's metabolic furnace to operate at a high enough level to compensate for cold-stress. In combination with a mixed browse diet,

In northern deer yards, perhaps the most nutritious browse whitetails may find is white cedar. This species offers an energy-rich fodder, and, where cedar trees are dense, provide excellent protective cover.

When the first blanket of snow covers the north and other nutritious vegetation is absent or no longer available to deer, they will switch from feeding on low-growing succulent plants to browsing on woody vegetation.

Deer in southern portions of the whitetail's range have a greater variety of plants available to them year-round, and even feed on succulent plants such as prickly pear cactus.

energy-rich agricultural crops provide deer with excellent nutrition and permit them to survive in relatively poor shelter.

In southern areas where infrequent snow occurs, favorite winter foods of whitetails are spurge, birdsfoot trefoil, chickweed, clovers, vetch, numerous broad-leaf plants, and a variety of grasses. Important browse species include coralberry, greenbrier, honeysuckle, bearberry, vaccinium, dewberry and supplejack, plus a host of other species that vary in availability and importance from one area to the next.

Although woody browse will represent the major winter forage of deer on northern range, deer prefer to feed on the more-succulent low-growing herbaceous plants such as sheep sorrel, hawkweed, strawberry, trefoil, lespediza, wintergreen and lichens, along with grasses and sedges that remain green beneath snow cover. As long as snow-free patches are available, deer will continue to search for and consume these more-nutritious foods, and in some areas they will paw through shallow snow cover to find them.

Even scant snow cover, however, may force deer to shift from eating nutritious herbaceous forage to less-nourishing woody browse. In southern Michigan's George Reserve Deer Research Area, for example, Bruce Coblentz observed that grasses and forbs comprised nearly half of the deer's winter diet when snow cover was absent, but declined sharply to zero when covered by a mere three inches of snow. In some high density deer herds, fawns have been reported to starve during winter when unable to obtain herbaceous food due to icy crusted snow.

Nonetheless, deer will paw through a foot or more of snow to feed upon acorns and beechnuts where these highly nutritious morsels are available. In winter on northern range, acorns and beechnuts are about the only natural foods available to whitetails that can match the high-energy content of farm crops. Acorns and beechnuts are especially high in fat and carbohydrates, and they contain significant amounts of crude protein, calcium, phosphorous, and certain vitamins.

Acorns and beechnuts are also important autumn foods for deer because they promote fattening. When abundantly available, a deer will eat about a pound and a half of acorns per day per one hundred pounds of body weight. Deer seem to prefer white oak acorns, but they will also eagerly consume the acorns of pin oak, red oak, black oak, and scrub oak. Unfortunately, annual crops of acorns and beechnuts are not dependable, nor are they always available to deer in winter. Acorn production during some years may amount to over 500 pounds per acre, but may be as low as only a few pounds per acre

during poor mast production years.

An acorn shortage sometimes creates special nutritional hardship for deer in certain areas. Even in the Midwest's oak-hickory forest region (centered in portions of Oklahoma, Missouri, Arkansas, Illinois, Tennessee, Indiana, Ohio and Kentucky), some deer are very dependent upon a good supply of acorns for autumn fattening and winter survival. During unusually harsh winters following poor acorn production there, deer sometimes suffer from a prolonged negative energy balance, and does in poor physical condition may then

Whereas whitetails will stop feeding on nutritious greens once the plants are covered with even a light blanket of snow, they will dig through considerable snow cover to obtain acorns and beechnuts.

experience poor survival of their newborn fawns the following spring.

In the Upper Great Lakes region, where most winters are nutritionally challenging for white-tailed deer, acorns periodically provide a valuable supplement to otherwise poor quality browse diets. In Michigan, for example, penned deer research revealed that deer fed diets of jack pine, oak browse, or balsam fir would not have been able to survive a 90-day period if they had not been supplemented with a mere one-half pound of acorns, daily, per one hundred pounds of body weight.

It's difficult to generalize about the whitetail's winter diet. What deer eat during this season varies greatly from area to area. Given the opportunity, however, deer will sample just about every tree and shrub within reach. Although they possess the inherent ability to select the best foods available, according to Ullrey, ". . . it is unlikely that deer possess nutritional wisdom." In other words, when quality food is scarce, deer will consume just about any kind of food, even if it is very woody, difficult to digest, and of low nutritive value.

Northern white cedar is about the only natural browse that, by itself, will sustain deer through a 100-day-plus yarding season on northern range. But even small amounts of cedar in the whitetail's winter diet tend to complement and improve the digestibility of other less nourishing browse species. Unfortunately, most northern white cedar deer yards are now severely overbrowsed, or the cedar has grown out of the deer's reach. Today, few areas exist where deer can adequately consume such high-quality forage on a daily basis.

In the absence of high-energy foods such as acorns or white cedar, diet diversity is the key to the survival of deer dependent upon woody browse during winter. While considered preferred browse species individually, red maple, sugar maple, striped maple,

Where locally abundant, acorns are an important component of the whitetail's fall and winter diet. In years when oaks produce poor mast crops, newborn fawns suffer depressed survival rates.

Wherever and whenever possible, whitetails seek diversity in their diet. Fruit trees such as these apples, much to the dismay of silviculturists, are magnets for hungry deer, especially in spring when whitetails favor the succulent fruit-bearing buds.

When too many deer concentrate in yarding areas, even where vegetation with high nutrient values is present, heavy feeding will create browse lines beyond the reach of many deer.

hazel, sumac, dogwood, and birch, among others, fail to meet the whitetail's winter nutritional requirements. In order to sustain deer through winter, these browse species must be eaten in combination or along with other high-energy foods. In contrast, species such as balsam fir, spruce, or pine are generally considered starvation foods, as they are very difficult for deer to digest and commonly represent the bulk of the rumen contents of starved deer.

It is important to note, however, that the low digestibility of certain forages does not reflect the true value of the forage, which may contribute certain important nutrients otherwise missing in the deer's diet. For example, some plants are too low in calcium, phosphorus, nitrogen or other nutrients but may be utilized if combined with other plants that provide the deficient elements. As a result, eating certain plants may aid in the digestion of others.

The most nutritious portions of woody browse are the tender tips of the plants' branches that have grown over the previous growing season. However, famished deer may browse these preferred sprouts repeatedly, eating them back to thumb-sized diameter, in some cases producing a "witch's broom" visual effect on the browsed plant. Starving deer may even resort to eating bark from large-diameter trees.

After many years of deer overabundance, the preferred trees and shrubs within heavily used deer wintering areas will show a distinct browse line where deer have eaten all the live foliage as high as they can reach. A browse line on preferred species such as white cedar is quite common, but such evidence on starvation foods like balsam fir, spruce, or pine warns of the potential for serious malnutrition among the area's resident deer.

STARVATION

In the North, high deer density and poor fawn growth rates, coupled with winter stress and food deprivation, often contribute to high overwinter mortality of small fawns even during those winters of only moderate severity. In Upper Michigan, high winter mortality of whitetails in areas with more than 50 deer per square mile on summer range is no longer a rare event: It has become commonplace.

Certainly, some deer are likely to die from malnutrition on northern range each winter. Historically, however, ever since the white man altered natural habitats and reduced or eliminated major predators that once held deer populations in check, the annual deer die-off has periodically been staggering. In northern Michigan alone, winter stress claimed an

estimated 117,000 deer in 1994; 125,000 in 1986; 67,000 in 1982; 100,000 in 1979; and over 115,000 in 1956. Michigan isn't the only state that has experienced excessive overwinter deer losses. Every state in the Upper Great Lakes region and in the Northeast, as well as the southern provinces of Canada, has recorded massive deer die-offs during certain winters. By some estimates, as many as two million whitetails died nationally during some severe winters in the 1950s.

The reasons deer die in winter aren't always clear. Obviously, not all of them die from starvation. Some are shot illegally; some die from hunting season wounds or

Death among whitetails in winter is a natural occurrence on northern range. Some years, deer mortality is moderate; other years, particularly during tough winters, it may be massive. Fawns usually represent the bulk of overwinter deer losses.

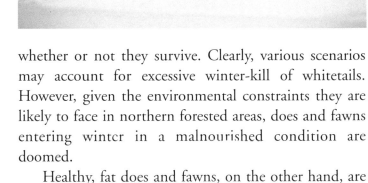

naturally incurred injuries; others die in accidents or from disease, and still more (especially malnourished ones) fall victim to predators. Nonetheless, the highest losses always occur during severe winters, and most deer die, either directly or indirectly, due to malnutrition. The evidence rests in their fat-depleted carcasses, where even the last energy reserves have been drawn from the cores of their bones, leaving a red gelatinous material where the marrow was once white with fat.

For does and fawns, the amount of body fat they accumulate prior to winter, and the amount of digestible browse available to them during winter, will determine whether or not they survive. Clearly, various scenarios may account for excessive winter-kill of whitetails. However, given the environmental constraints they are likely to face in northern forested areas, does and fawns entering winter in a malnourished condition are doomed.

Healthy, fat does and fawns, on the other hand, are reasonably well equipped to withstand several months of severe winter weather, even when faced with moderate food deprivation. Body fat is especially important because it serves as reserve energy. If deer are on a negative energy balance, which is normally the case for

Does and fawns entering winter with adequate layers of fat can be expected to survive a moderately harsh winter season. Given a desolate, protracted winter, though, their chances of living to spring break-up can quickly dwindle.

Those that enter winter with maximum fat reserves can usually withstand upwards of 30 percent weight loss without dying. This is not to imply that complete depletion of fat stores during winter is normal, necessary, or a wise strategy. Nutritional stress may very well carry into the spring period, even after snowmelt, requiring reserve energy to compensate for periodic unexpected nutritional shortages. Surplus fat can always be "dumped," or flushed from the system, when lush food is plentiful.

Bill Mautz, who has conducted extensive research on deer physiology at the University of New Hampshire, likens the annual fat cycle of deer to a sled ride down a brushy hillside. At the bottom of the hill is a sharp drop and potential death from starvation. Deer must first climb the hill during summer and autumn, building fat along the way. The amount of fat stored prior to winter, which will depend upon range conditions and bodily requirements, will determine how high the animal is able to climb on the hill, and hence, the length of its ride down; the longer the ride, the better the chance of surviving until spring. Winter browse availability is depicted in the analogy as brush on the hillside. Food in the form of woody browse will not completely stop the deer's downhill ride but will serve to slow the rate of descent—slowing the rate of fat depletion and, thereby,

northern deer during winter, the body tissue is utilized to help meet their basic energy needs. Accelerated catabolism of body protein occurs simultaneously with fat mobilization; the greater the dietary energy deficiency, the more rapid the degradation of body protein. However, deer can not survive winter on body reserves alone. In fact, its doubtful if a healthy adult doe could live for more than 45 to 60 days without food in winter, regardless of how fat she was at the start.

Some weight loss by northern deer during winter is normal. Even well-nourished adult does and fawns are likely to lose 10 to 15 percent of their body weight.

Entering winter in good physical condition and with adequate fat stores, does and fawns may lose a tenth of their weight during an easy winter, and up to a third of their autumn weight—before dying—during a severe winter season.

The hump-backed posture of extremely malnourished deer indicates they have reached a nutritional point of no return. Given quality food at this stage, they will be unable to withstand the metabolic stress of feeding.

increasing the prospects for survival. Each deer gets just one sled ride each winter. If it is lucky, it will stop before reaching the bottom of the hill and falling off the end.

Healthy whitetails are quite capable of withstanding severe weather and food deprivation during January and February, when they're geared-down physiologically and adjusted behaviorally to endure great adversity. It is prolonged winters—ones that start in November or early December, extend into April, and overlap periods of high energy demand—that can be so devastating to deer. The whitetail's impressive adaptations for winter survival diminish in value around mid-March. Thereafter,

steadily increasing food demands render deer once again exceedingly sensitive to environmental stress factors.

Death from malnutrition is an insidious, pathetically slow process. Fat depletion and physical weakening progress with nearly undetectable signs, until it's too late for recovery. In the final stages, however, a deer's coat roughens, its hip bones show, and hollows appear in its flanks. The starving animal spends most of its time bedded down, in a curled head-to-tail position to minimize body surface exposure. It adopts a lethargic, uncaring attitude, no longer bounding away, flag waving, as danger nears. Small deer, especially, stand hump-backed, their front legs spread slightly, back legs close together, and hold their head up at a 45 degree angle. Deer so weakened become easy prey for predators—a sudden and merciful fate compared to a lingering death from starvation.

Investigations conducted at Pennsylvania State University under the direction of Truman Hersberger and Charles Cushwa revealed that each deer has a certain starvation threshold beyond which it can no longer survive even though feed is available. Physically stressed animals, in particular, incurred irreversible damage to their rumen lining, and their rumen microflora lost its ability to digest cellulose. At some unknown time during starvation, rumen attrition and adrenal exhaustion became irreversible. Thereafter, a deer so stressed could no longer handle the metabolic stress of feeding.

The work at Penn State exemplified that harassment and physical exertion tend to speed-up the adverse effects of malnutrition and lower a deer's starvation threshold. A sudden heavy energy demand, for whatever reason, may kill a deer even through its energy reserves are not completely exhausted. Harassment by dogs, unusually cold weather, or exceptionally strenuous travel conditions during late winter, for example, could have especially devastating effects on malnourished deer and lead to the death of some that might otherwise have survived.

Although some small deer may succumb to malnutrition early in winter, most deer starve during March and April. Fawns lose body weight faster than adults and usually are the first to die. Fawn mortality normally comprises 50 to 90 percent of overwinter deaths, but the age composition of the losses tends to vary, depending upon severity of winter weather, nutritional conditions during summer and autumn, and availability of quality food within the wintering area.

Based upon his examination of over 1,800 winter-killed deer in the central Adirondack region of New York during the 1930s and 1940s, William Severinghaus found nearly two-thirds were fawns, about four percent were yearlings, 10 percent were prime-age deer (from

two to seven years old), and 23 percent were older animals. During the years studied, losses were heavier among females than males for all age classes.

Extremely heavy winter deer losses have also been reported in parts of Canada. During the severe winter of 1958-59, for example, investigators found about 37 dead deer per square mile in certain deer yards surveyed in Ontario. They estimated that 47 percent of the wintering deer herd perished. The next winter was mild, however, and only about nine percent of the deer died. Field studies in Quebec during the early 1970s revealed comparably high death rates for wintering whitetails,

Most starvation-related mortality occurs in late winter, and fawns comprise the bulk of those losses. In early winter, few deer die from starvation, but those that do are almost always young-of-the-year.

ranging annually from 20 to 50 percent of the wintering populations. Francois Potvin and his coworkers concluded, however, that such heavy mortality rates resulted from extremely severe winter conditions, not because of deer overabundance or lack of food.

Most deer populations are heavily hunted, so few deer live longer than 10 years in the wild. Old-age bucks and does are also highly susceptible to winter stress; few does in excess of 16 years old or bucks older than 12 years are likely to survive tough northern winters. The oldest free-ranging deer ever reported was a 20-year-old doe shot in New York. Probably the oldest free-ranging buck ever reported was a 17-year-old live-trapped by Nelson and Mech in northern Minnesota. I recorded 11 does in the Petrel Grade Deer Yard that lived beyond 10 years, one being nearly 17 years old when I last saw her. The oldest buck, however, an extremely emaciated 12-year-old, was killed by coyotes during January.

Adult bucks deviate from the highly adaptive fat cycle exhibited by does and fawns. Healthy does and fawns can rely upon 20 to 30 percent of their body weight for reserve energy during the winter period. Bucks, on the other hand, exhaust most of their energy reserves during the autumn rut, leaving them very lean for a four- to five-month stretch encompassing all of the winter season.

Certainly, it's not unexpected that some bucks, battle-scarred and injured while fighting during autumn, occasionally fall easy prey to alert predators or succumb later to their injuries and malnutrition. In fact, its more of a mystery how so many bucks in such seemingly wretched physical condition can survive the stressful winter season.

There is little consensus among investigators regarding buck mortality rates over winter. In some areas, bucks seem to experience disproportionately high overwinter death rates among adult deer, while in other areas it's the adult female segment of the population that appears more vulnerable to winter stress. The reasons for such difference tend to rest in deer density and range conditions. In areas of extremely high deer density and resultant overbrowsed range, adult males are more likely to succumb to winter malnutrition than adult females, but the reverse is generally true in better nourished, low density herds.

Although seemingly handicapped in winter because of their scant fat stores, the buck's large body size contributes to greater metabolic efficiency and ability to withstand greater cold-stress. The size of the rumen in relation to body size will determine the quality of forage that can be digested; the larger the body size, the lower the basal metabolic rate per unit of body weight. Adult

*On most northern deer ranges, winter mortality can be higher among bucks
or does, depending on deer population densities and availability of food.
Regardless of other factors, does require higher-quality foods than do bucks.*

In the North, most bucks cast their antlers in December or January; bucks in the South retain theirs as late as April. The timing of antler loss is dictated by testosterone levels.

bucks normally weight about 30 percent more than females (but the spread narrows when summer nutrition is poor) and have a lower whole-body metabolic requirement per unit of gut capacity. This difference permits bucks to subsist on lower-quality foods when nutritious ones are scarce, a real benefit during winter. Also, since large-bodied bucks are better equipped to withstand cold-stress (Bergmann's Rule), they can occupy winter habitat separate from does and fawns where the shelter may be relatively poor but the supply of browse is better.

Within a given region, the timing of a white-tailed buck's antler casting (drop) will provide a reasonably good indication of his general health status; prolonged antler retention is indicative of good health. Antlers are cast when blood levels of the male hormone testosterone decline, which in turn are dependent upon the buck's dominance rank and physical condition. Because antler casting is under hormonal control, a buck may drop both of his antlers on the same day, possibly only minutes apart, or, more rarely, carry one antler a week or longer than the other. I observed one buck that had been injured while fighting drop his antlers a month apart.

In the north, where bucks generally drop antlers from mid-December to late January, some bucks drop their antlers on summer range, and others carry them into wintering areas. Large old dominant bucks tend to drop their antlers earlier than do small young subordinates. In the Midwest, where antler casting extends from January to late March, bucks with large antlers reportedly retain them longer than do bucks with small antlers. By comparison, in the South, where breeding seasons are prolonged, some bucks may retain their antlers until March or April, and large-antlered bucks there tend to carry antlers later than small-antlered ones.

It is important to note, though, that it is not latitude per se that causes the north-to-south difference in the timing of antler casting. A buck's nutrition and general health status, as well as his dominance rank and length of the breeding season, interact to determine the time and order in which he casts his antlers. We demonstrated, for example, that artificially raising the nutritional level of our enclosed herd at Cusino via supplemental feeding greatly delayed antler casting and caused many bucks,

especially those two and a half years old, to carry their antlers until March or, in some instances, even into April. Improved nutrition for our northern bucks, then, produced an antler casting schedule more closely resembling that of southern whitetails, even though the breeding schedule of enclosure does was not prolonged.

Prime-age does entering winter in a healthy and well-fattened condition are without doubt the hardiest of all age and sex classes of whitetails. In winter, they die from malnutrition only under the most stressful conditions imaginable. For deer wintering in the Petrel Grade Deer Yard, for instance, the winter of 1964-65 was ravaging. An estimated 142 deer died in a single square-mile of the deer yard I studied. Although fawns and old does represented most of the losses, even prime-age does died that April. In the final tally, prime-age does comprised more than one-third of the adult does I found that had starved or were killed by predators.

Bucks may cast both of their antlers almost simultaneously, but only rarely. As is more often the case, male deer will "lose" their antlers anywhere from a few hours to a week apart.

The effects of such a severe winter are really twofold, of course, because malnutrition among pregnant does during the latter third of gestation, in particular, contributes to poor fetal growth and, ultimately, to high infant mortality rates. Whitetail does rarely abort or resorb fetuses. Instead, when malnourished, they tend to produce dead or underweight fawns. Most fawns are born alive, but stunted individuals—generally those under five pounds in weight—usually die within 48 hours. Such losses due to malnutrition may be negligible following mild winters but may claim more than 70 percent of the fawn crop following an especially severe winter.

DEER YARD CUTTINGS

During winter, timber cutting conducted in the vicinity of overgrown or browsed-out deer yards commonly attract large concentrations of deer that feed upon the felled browse. Because white cedar is a highly nutritious deer browse, logging in conifer swamps containing cedar can be highly beneficial to resident deer. An abundant supply of browse in close proximity to protective cover allows deer to minimize energy expenditures when traveling from resting sites to feeding locations. Typically, clear-cutting an acre of mature white cedar swamp yields around 5,000 pounds of nutritious browse, enough to feed 10 to 15 deer for a 100-day winter period. When carefully planned and conducted, then, winter logging can permit far more deer to survive than the habitat might otherwise naturally produce or support.

Timber cutting in deer wintering areas can be highly beneficial or, in the long-run, sometimes may be very detrimental to whitetails. Carefully planned cuttings provide immediate food for deer from the tops of felled trees, and re-growth of the removed vegetation can provide a fairly prolonged food supply for deer. Poorly planned cuts, however, can lead to eventual destruction of the conifers' winter

When deer become famished in winter, they gravitate to timber cuts to feed on freshly felled conifers. Near active cutting operations, deer quickly associate the sound of a chain saw with the presence of food.

Small-scale clearcuts can provide whitetails with nutritious food when they need it most, but poorly executed cuts result in long-term deprivation of food and winter shelter.

Revegetation of cutover areas provide deer with some food in later years, but rarely does white cedar regenerate to its original densities. Deer thus lose thermal cover provided by thick stands of the conifers.

thermal cover because the cutover sites regenerate to deciduous species that provide deer with less protection.

The problems involved in managing white cedar stands are numerous and appear especially difficult to solve. Few cedar swamp deer yards are currently being cut and managed specifically to rehabilitate them as deer wintering areas. On private lands, cutting of white cedar often proceeds with little or no regard for the future well-being of wintering whitetails. In fact, some cedar growth is cut and intentionally replanted to other more-marketable species.

Meanwhile, primarily because wildlife managers and foresters disagree among themselves as to which logging procedures should be employed, or because they fear intensive browsing at present day high deer densities will preclude any chances of re-establishing the highly preferred cedar in cutover areas, many biologists oppose logging of deer yards on public lands. For a combination of reasons, the cedar swamp acreage in Wisconsin alone has already declined by about 75 percent since 1850. Eastern hemlock, another species that provides prime thermal cover for whitetails, has also been greatly reduced in the northern lake states.

Frequently, winter logging operations are also detrimental to deer because the browse provided is of poor quality or limited in quantity. Cuttings initiated

early in winter sometimes lure deer into new yarding locations, areas that otherwise would be unfavorable if not for an abundance of felled browse. If such logging terminates before deer are able to leave the area, hungry deer may become stranded, and large numbers of whitetails may starve before spring arrives.

SUPPLEMENTAL FEEDING

Large-scale artificial feeding of whitetails to prevent starvation has also been attempted in many northern areas. Initially, most of these ventures were rather poorly conceived, done on an emergency basis, and offered

Supplemental feeding of whitetails, if done under strict guidelines, can be beneficial. Done under emergency conditions, as is often the case, it can be detrimental to the herd, even lethal to some animals.

limited amounts of relatively poor quality feed to animals already on the verge of death. Often, horrendous losses still occur, and in some cases feeding high-quality foods to starving animals merely contributes to the problem and causes additional mortality.

Most wildlife managers discourage artificial feeding of whitetails, with good cause. Although suitable pelletized rations have been developed and are readily available from feed mills, a strong case against supplemental feeding of wild deer rests on economics, practicality, and potential damage to the range when feeding guidelines are not followed closely or deer

Feeding whitetails may help keep them in good condition if they aren't already malnourished. However, deer should be provided specially formulated rations, and humans should avoid conditioning deer to human presence.

population size is not carefully regulated by hunter harvesting of surplus animals.

Many well-meaning people insist upon feeding deer foods of questionable nutritive value, assuming that "every little bit helps." As a sole diet, however, sugar beets, apples, potatoes, lettuce, rutabagas, corn, bread, or chocolate cake fail to meet the whitetail's basic nutritional requirements. Likewise, hay provides little nourishment for deer unless it's good second-cut alfalfa or fine clover. Even then, deer are likely to waste more of the hay than they eat. A balanced diet might occasionally be achieved if these individual poor-quality foods are provided throughout winter in great variety and quantity, along with a mixed supply of natural browse. The chances of accidentally striking upon an ideal combination, however, are quite remote at best, and feeding of "table-scrap-variety" foods to deer may do more damage than good.

In order for deer to digest high-energy foods, they must be in relatively good physical condition and harbor healthy rumen microflora. Starving deer generally exhibit altered rumen function due to decreased concentrations of rumen microflora and volatile fatty acids, and they may not be able to digest high-energy foods containing readily fermentable carbohydrates. When a starving deer consumes large quantities of a energy-rich food such as corn, for example, potentially toxic quantities of lactic acid may accumulate in the rumen. Such problems arose in Michigan in the 1960s when biologists documented increased mortality among malnourished deer that had been fed corn.

Supplemental feeding of healthy deer throughout winter is entirely another matter and far different from emergency feeding of famished deer. Although pelletized rations formulated to meet the whitetail's basic nutritional requirements serve the animal best, even small amounts of high energy farm crops may readily complement a well balanced browse diet and help maintain deer in excellent physical condition. Today, people often resort to backyard feeding of whitetails, with apparent success, thereby encouraging wintering deer populations to form even in residential areas where no deer would likely survive without human assistance.

This is not to imply that artificial feeding of deer, as commonly occurs today in many residential areas, is a wise practice, nor is "taming" of deer necessarily ethical where deer populations are regulated by hunting. Research conducted by Rongstad and Lewis in northern Wisconsin revealed that supplementally fed does, in particular, tend to be more vulnerable to hunting. Also, deer do not readily distinguish the browse provided by ornamental trees and shrubbery from that growing wild

in the nearby countryside, and they can soon become destructive nuisances when the handouts do not completely fulfill their needs. In fact, conditioning deer to human attention and artificial diets, often for purely human enjoyment, frequently reduces the status of the otherwise elegant whitetail to that of a "pest."

During the 1970s, in the square-mile Cusino enclosure, we conducted a comprehensive study to evaluate the pros and cons of supplementally feeding whitetails. Provided that certain strict feeding guidelines are adhered to, we found that supplementing whitetails' natural browse diets throughout winter with a well balanced pelletized

Supplemental feeding of whitetails in residential areas often maintains their presence in areas they otherwise would not inhabit. Drawbacks to this include increased deer mortality from vehicle collisions.

Providing deer feed in areas where they exceed the carrying capacity of the summer range can later lead to cataclysmic mortality when the herd grows beyond the land's capacity to support it outside of winter.

ration tends to reduce overwinter deer mortality while helping improve their reproductive success. Supplemental feeding permits a higher population than the habitat can support under natural conditions, however, and can contribute to a rapid, if not startling, deer population growth rate. These findings were generally substantiated by Rongstad and Lewis for free-ranging deer in northern Wisconsin.

Under no conditions, though, should a winter deer feeding program be initiated where the local deer herd already exceeds the carrying capacity of the summer range or where a significant harvest of surplus antlerless deer can not be achieved. Without fail, mortality soars and biological returns drop sharply when the artificially managed deer herd grows to excessive size.

Many private hunting clubs feed deer regularly in winter in hopes of providing plentiful healthy hunting stock. Most of these efforts fail miserably, however, because of insufficient antlerless deer harvesting, which results in deer population levels higher than the summer range can favorably support.

Some provinces of Canada, including Alberta, Manitoba, Ontario, and Saskatchewan currently employ winter feeding of whitetails as part of their on-going deer management programs. Some of these programs are the result of political pressure, as they have been in Michigan,

Wisconsin, Minnesota, and probably other northern states. Most state and provincial game management agencies provide private citizens with technical advice on when, where, what, and how to feed whitetails, but the agencies themselves avoid becoming involved in the actual feeding of deer.

In Manitoba and Saskatchewan, winter deer feeding is designed primarily to mitigate damage to farm forage (usually hay bales). Where deer are causing damage to farm forage, provincial managers place feeders filled with nutritious pelletized feed near deer bedding cover. In effect, these feeders are situated between deer and the foraging problem and thereby intercept deer and eliminate the damage problem.

In response to severe conditions during the 1988-89 winter, the Minnesota Department of Natural Resources initiated a large-scale emergency deer feeding program, distributing nearly 4,000 tons of pelletized feed over 46,000 square miles of deer range at a cost of over one million dollars. Nonetheless, the emergency program was largely unsuccessful because most of the supplemental feed was unused by deer and, thus, wasted. In spite of the effort, deer populations declined as a result of increased mortality of fawns and reduced production of fawns the following spring.

Past experience indicates that emergency feeding of

Where agricultural crops are available to deer in winter, even small quantities of energy-rich food such as corn will provide adequate nutrition to whitetails living primarily upon browse.

deer is risky, is impractical in remote areas, but is sometimes feasible in accessible areas. The most successful artificial feeding programs will be those where deer have been conditioned to artificial feeds over a period of years and are provided unlimited access to nutritious rations throughout winter. For an artificial feeding program to be successful, deer population size also must be closely regulated through hunting, to maintain deer numbers below carrying capacity of the summer range. Needless to say, examples of such successes are rare.

THE "PECK ORDER"

When high-quality browse or rich supplemental feed is concentrated and limited, large numbers of hungry deer may congregate and compete aggressively for the limited food. In some cases, deer competing in these aggregations expend more energy than is gained through the food consumed. Such intense social strife and fighting among whitetails generally leads to a strict dominance hierarchy, or "peck order," wherein each deer establishes a certain social rank. Achieving a dominant position assures three things: better access to limited food, maintenance of superior physical condition, and improved chances for survival.

While investigating the aggressive behavior of whitetails at winter cuttings, I identified seven basic ag-

When food is limited, dominant individuals in the herd will have the greatest access to it. Rank is established over other animals through aggressive behavior such as flailing, seen here.

gressive physical actions employed by deer when establishing dominance. These include the (1) ear-drop, (2) hard-look, (3) sidle, (4) rush, (5) snorting, (6) strike, and (7) flail. Most encounters started with direct eye contact, followed by the stereotyped ear-drop hard-look combination, which terminated aggressive interactions in about 25 percent of the conflicts I observed.

If neither animal will back away, however, the dominant individual then might strike the subordinate, sometimes rather half-heartedly, with a foreleg. Very aggressive individuals may lunge or rush in stiff-legged fashion at an adversary, striking out with one or both forelegs while emitting a snort, which seems to enhance the effectiveness of the charge.

The ultimate form of combat employed between antlerless whitetails is the flail, which normally involves two closely matched individuals and probably more often occurs between combat-experienced adult deer rather than fawns. When neither individual acknowledges submission to lesser-threat postures, the two animals then rise on their hind legs and flail at each other with their forefeet. Only about four percent of the 400 conflicts I recorded ever reached this intensity, and each of those incidents lasted only a few seconds before the subordinate deer dropped to a normal stance and retreated.

Unlike aggressive interactions between deer during

Ears laid back, two evenly matched whitetails approach each other until one strikes out with a foreleg, striking the other deer in the throat. Such encounters usually do not result in serious injury.

other times of the year, dominant whitetails seldom chase subordinates any distance when jockeying for favored feeding positions at winter cuttings. Instead, the interactions seem to serve primarily for dominating favored feeding positions. Frequently, even when in fairly close contact with a more-dominant individual, subordinate deer can circumvent serious conflict by avoiding eye contact and merely moving aside at the approach of the dominant individual.

Surprisingly, even when hundreds of deer are congregated at a cutting, individuals seem to be able to recognize one another, to recall previous conflicts with other deer, and soon realize their social rank within the herd. Although the frequency of threat posturing tends to increase among hungry deer towards late winter, the frequency of potentially injurious (and energetically costly) striking and flailing decreases as winter progresses. Consequently, the firm dominance hierarchy that develops not only benefits the most-dominant individuals, it also helps to conserve energy among all deer when food resources are scarce.

Within the established dominance hierarchy, adult bucks (those two and a half years old and older) typically dominate all other deer, while adult does dominate fawns. Prime-age does usually rank just below the large males, whereas does older than 12 years, and yearlings of both sexes, tend to rank just ahead of most male fawns. Smaller doe fawns usually hold the lowest rank.

It's important to note, however, that top-ranked individuals seldom show aggression towards smaller subordinates that maintain submissive postures. Also, very low-ranked fawns or even some young does may benefit from being closely associated with a high-ranked female relative, thereby gaining better access to limited food. Therefore, although fawns generally suffer the most from competition for limited food and comprise the bulk of malnutrition-related deaths, a surprising number of them may survive prolonged winters at logging operations or artificial feeding sites.

BREAK-UP

If whitetails occasionally experience "psychological highs"—and I think they probably do—one such high time for northern subspecies must be during the spring break-up, when snow finally melts and gives way to fresh sprouts of nutritious herbaceous forage. And just as healthy spotted fawns play and frolic, so do feisty adult deer cavort after surviving a harsh winter.

Perhaps such seemingly neurotic behavior has a physiological basis due to the sudden surge of energy-rich food that once again fuels the whitetail's metabolic furnace to capacity. Maybe that extra energy just naturally allows for frivolous behavior—like racing about, kicking, and jumping into the air, for no apparent reason—otherwise not affordable during the depressing months of winter.

The "walking dead"—malnourished animals with irreversible damage to their digestive systems—will leave the confines of their winter homes too, but with far less exuberance than others that gorge on the lush new growth that spring brings forth. For those whitetails that surpassed their starvation threshold, the flush of nutritious forage comes too late. Their systems can no longer handle the chores associated with digestion, and there is no hope of recovery. Ironically, the ravages of winter will follow some of them many miles to the bountiful greenery of their summer ranges, where they may linger a while, then die.

Sometimes, of course, the bones and hides of deer strewn along manure-paved trails within wintering cover already stand as mute evidence of the stressful winter season. Nearby, ravens perch and squawk, signaling that all is not well in the local deer yards. Humans may articulate reasons, oftentimes weak ones, for excessive winter deer die-offs from one area to another, but the real causes, generally, are simply the result of too many deer for the amount of food and cover available.

Pregnant does that venture from the wintering grounds carry with them the next generation—embryos nearly three-quarters grown—and hold the key to deer abundance in the months ahead. Until spring break-up, the unborn, looking every bit like miniature newborn fawns with spotted coats and floppy ears, have been nurtured primarily by the reserves of their mother's body. Unfortunately, some of the unborn may already show the signs of malnutrition; those grossly undersized late in gestation will not recover sufficiently to survive.

The fate of other unborn fawns is still undetermined. If food, cover, and weather conditions are favorable, prospective mothers may be able to consume enough nutritious forage to meet the fantastic demands of the rapidly growing fetuses, not to mention the

When a pregnant doe leaves her winter yard, the fetus she carries is three-quarters grown. By now, the fate of the unborn fawn is sealed. If the doe suffered severe malnutrition during winter, chance of the fawn surviving or even being born alive is small.

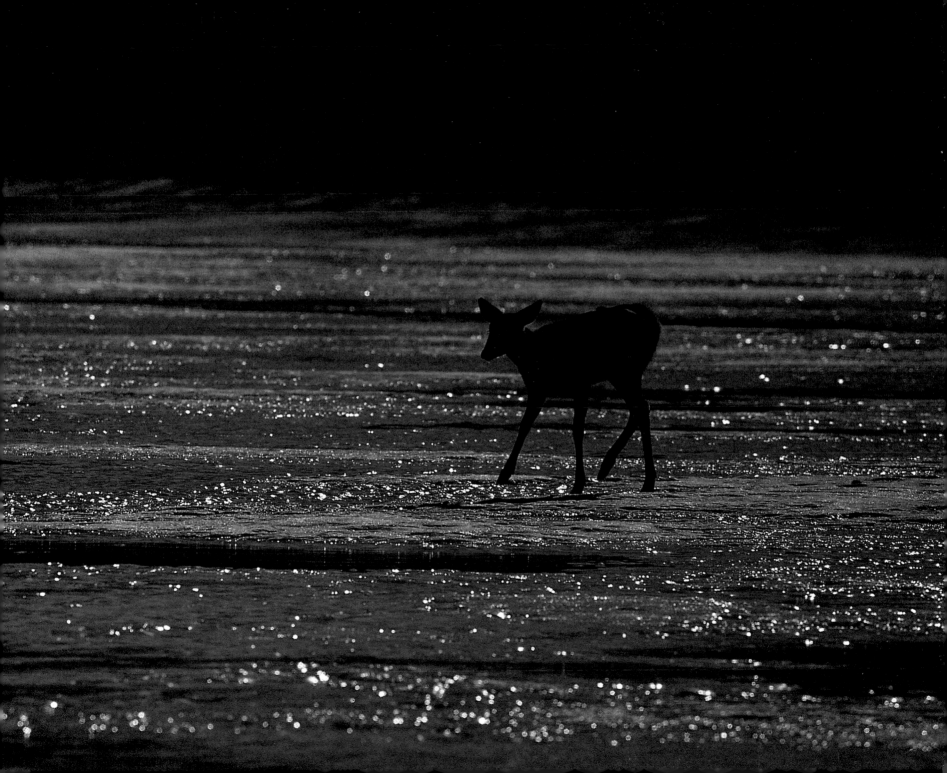

Whitetail mortality due to severe winter weather is sometimes unavoidable. With adequate food and cover, however, many will still survive. Human failure to properly manage habitat and deer numbers are the primary reasons for persistent losses.

enormous energy that will be required later to nourish the newborn. Unborn fawns whose mothers face less favorable conditions, not uncommon on northern range during spring, may not be so fortunate. For them, the cost of inadequate nutrition during the late stages of gestation will result in poor fetal growth and high infant death rates.

Sometimes excessive winter die-offs of deer and subsequent poor fawn rearing success due to exceptionally fierce winters are unavoidable. Within the whitetail's range, however, exceptionally fierce winters occur only periodically. Given adequate shelter and a reasonably good food supply, the healthy whitetail is well equipped to withstand periodic spells of severe winter weather. So, one should not too often make excuses that dwell on the idea of unavoidable losses in order to explain routine massive overwinter losses and chronic reproductive failures of whitetails living in northern environments. Such maladies are more often the product of human error.

THE FUTURE

In many northern areas, mismanagement of whitetail populations or their habitat have been far more devastating than the effects of periodic severe winter weather. Insufficient deer harvesting or disproportionate harvesting of the sexes has led to deer overabundance as well as herd composition imbalances, overbrowsing, and accelerated habitat deterioration. In other cases, the combination of human encroachment and poor forestry practices have fragmented, failed to regenerate, or outright purposely destroyed valuable winter habitat for whitetails.

Some of these management shortcomings may be remedied in the future, depending upon economics, resource management emphasis, and public education. It can only be hoped that the hunting and non-hunting public will become more cognizant of the need to control deer populations through proper harvesting practices and be more willing to support scientifically sound harvest strategies.

Throughout their range, too, the welfare of whitetails will continue to hinge heavily upon the availability of suitable habitat and its proper management. Human progress and changing farming practices will continue to impact the health and general well-being of whitetails wintering in mild climates. Meanwhile, changes in forest management intensity and

direction, in response to fluctuating demands for forest products and recreational land development, will likely create alternating patterns of feast or famine for deer in northern areas. These trends will probably continue to produce boom and bust whitetail populations, especially near the northern limits of the whitetail's geographic range—just as have occurred ever since the white man altered natural habitats and reduced or eliminated the natural predators that once held wintering whitetail populations in check.

Obviously, however, neither humanity nor nature are totally predictable. In the future, anti-hunting sentiments, changing attitudes among hunters, biodiversity management, global warming, as well as a host of other unforeseen factors could impact the welfare of whitetails throughout their current range. In that event, new challenges or unexpected opportunities could either diminish or enhance the resourceful whitetail's quality of life in the years ahead.

In the future, as in the past, whitetail numbers will be predicated on maintaining suitable habitat. Population sizes will also be determined by public acceptance of scientifically sound deer management policies.

SELECTED REFERENCES

Baker, R. H. 1983. *Michigan mammals.* Michigan State Univ. Press, East Lansing, MI. 642 pp.

Brown, B. A. 1974. Social organization in male groups of white-tailed deer. Pages 436-446 in V. Geist and F. Walther eds. The behavior of ungulates and its relation to management. *Int. Union Conserv. Nat. Pub. 24.* Morges, Switzerland. IUCN 940 pp.

Coblentz, B. E. 1970. Food habits of George Reserve deer. *J. Wildl. Manage.* 34:535-540.

Doepker, R. V., and J. J. Ozoga. 1991. Wildlife values of northern white-cedar. Pages 15-34 in D. O. Lantagne, ed. Northern white-cedar in Michigan. Mich. State Univ. Agri. Exp. Sta. Res. Rept. 512, Workshop Proc., Sault Ste. Marie. 122 pp.

Duvendeck, J. P. 1962. The value of acorns in the diet of Michigan deer. *J. Wildl. Manage.* 26:371-379.

Forand, K. J., R. L. Marchinton, and K. V. Miller. 1985. Influence of dominance rank on the antler cycle of white-tailed deer. *J. Mamm.* 66:58-62.

Geist, V. 1995. Mule deer and white-tailed deer beginnings. *Deer & Deer Hunting* 18(5):66-71.

Gill, J. D. 1957. Review of deer yard management 1956. *Game Div. Bull.* 5. Augusta: Maine Department of Inland Fish and Game. 61 pp.

Goss, R. J. 1983. *Deer antlers: regeneration, function, and evolution.* Academic Press, NY. 316 pp.

Habeck, J. R., and J. T. Curtis. 1959. Forest cover and deer population densities in early northern Wisconsin. Wisconsin Acad. Sci., Arts and Letters. 48:49-56.

Halls, L. K., ed. 1984. *White-tailed deer: ecology and management.* Wildl. Manage. Inst., The Stackpole Co., Harrisburg, PA. 870 pp.

Herschberger, T. V., and C. T. Cushwa. 1984. The effects offasting and refeeding on white-tailed deer. *Bull.* 846. Pennsylvania State Univer., University Park. 26 pp.

Hoffman, R. A., and P. F. Robinson. 1966. Changes in some endocrine glands of white-tailed deer as affected by season,sex and age. *J. Mammal.* 47:266-280.

Hoskinson, R. L., and L. D. Mech. 1976. White-tailed deer migration and its role in wolf predation. *J. Wildl. Manage.* 40:429-441.

Huegel, C. N. 1979. Winter ecology of coyotes in northern Wisconsin. M.Sc. Thesis, Univer. Wisconsin-Madison, 32 pp.

Huegel, C. N., and O. J. Rongstad. 1985. Winter foraging patterns and consumption rates of northern Wisconsin coyotes. *Amer. Midland Naturalist.* 113:203-207.

Johnston, W. F. 1977. Manager's handbook for northern white-cedar in the north central States. *U.S. For. Serv. Gen. Tech. Rep.* NC-35. 18 pp.

Kelsall, J. P. 1969. Structural adaptations of moose and deer for snow. *J. Mammal.* 50:302-310

Kleiber, M. 1961. *The fire of life: an introduction to animal energetics.* John Wiley and Sons, Inc., New York. 454 pp.

Krefting, L. W. 1969. The rise and fall of the coyote on Isle Royale. *Naturalist* 20:24-31.

Lewis, T. L. 1990. The effects of supplemental feeding on white-tailed deer in northwestern Wisconsin. Ph.D. Thesis, Univ. Wisconsin-Madison. 79 pp.

Lima, S. L., and L. M Dill. 1990. Behavioral decisions made under the risk of predation: a review and prospectus. *Canadian J. Zool.* 68:619-640.

Mautz, W. W. 1978. Sledding on a bushy hillside: the fat cycle in deer. *Wildl. Soc. Bull.* 6:88-90.

Mautz, W. W., J. Kanter, and P. J. Pekins. 1992. Seasonal metabolic rhythms of captive female white-tailed deer: a reexamination. *J. Wildl. Manage.* 56:656-661

McCullough, D. R. 1979. *The George Reserve deer herd.* Univ. Michigan Press, Ann Arbor. 271 pp.

McCullough, D. R., D. H. Hirth, and S. J. Newhouse. 1989. Resource partitioning between the sexes in white-tailed deer. *J. Wildl. Manage.* 53:277-283.

McCord, C. M. 1974. Selection of winter habitat by Bobcats *(Lynx rufus)* on the Quabbin Reservation, Massachusetts. *J. Mammal.* 55:428-437.

McDonald, S., and K. V. Miller. 1994. Reconstruction: How the South's deer herds were rebuilt. *Deer & Deer Hunting* 17(6):26-32.

Mech, L. D. 1977. Wolf-pack buffer zones as prey reservoirs. *Science* 198:320-321.

Mech, L. D., and P. D. Karns. 1977. Role of the wolf in a deer decline in the Superior National Forest. Res. Pap. NC-148. St. Paul: USDA Forest Service, N. Cent. For. Exp. Stn. 23 pp.

Messier, F., and C. Barrette. 1982. The social system of the coyote *(Canis latrans)* in a forested habitat. *Can. J. Zool.* 60:1743-1753.

Messier, F., and C. Barrette. 1983. The efficiency of yarding behaviour by white-tailed deer as an antipredator strategy. *Can. J. Zool.* 63:785-789.

Moen, A. N. 1968. Surface temperatures and radiant heat loss from white-tailed deer. *J. Wildl. Manage.* 32:338-344.

Moen, A. N. 1973. *Wildlife ecology.* San Franciso: W. H. Freeman and Co. 458 pp.

Moen, A. N. 1976. Energy exhange of white-tailed deer, western Minnesota. *Ecology* 57:192-198.

Nelson, M. E., and L. D. Mech. 1981. Deer social organization and wolf predation in northeastern Minnesota. *Wildl. Monogr.* 77. 53 pp.

Nelson, M. E., and L. D. Mech. 1986. Relationship between snow depth and gray wolf predation on white-tailed deer. *J. Wildl. Manage.* 50:471-474.

Nelson, M. E., and L. D. Mech. 1990. Weights, productivity, and mortality of old white-tailed deer. *J. Mammal.* 17:689-691.

Nelson, M. E., and L. D. Mech. 1991. Wolf predation risk associated with white-tailed deer movements. *Can. J. Zool.* 69:2696-2699.

Nero, R. W., and R. E. Wrigley. 1977. Status and habits of the cougar in Manitoba. *Canadian Field-Naturalist* 91:28-40.

Nixon, C. M., L. P. Hansen, and P. A. Brewer. 1988. Characteristics of winter habitats used by deer in Illinois. *J. Wildl. Manage.* 52:552-555.

Nixon, C. M., L. P. Hansen, P. A. Brewer, and J. E. Chelsvig. 1991. Ecology of white-tailed deer in an intensively farmed region of Illinois. *Wildl. Monogr.* 118. 77 pp.

Ozoga, J. J. 1968. Variations in microclimate in a conifer swamp deeryard in northern Michigan. *J. Wildl. Manage.* 32:574-585.

Ozoga, J. J. 1969. Some longevity records for female white-tailed deer in northern Michigan. *J. Wildl. Manage.* 33:1027-1028.

Ozoga, J. J. 1972. Aggressive behavior of white-tailed deer at winter cuttings. *J. Wildl. Manage.* 36:861-868.

Ozoga, J. J., and L. W. Gysel. 1972. Response of white-tailed deer to winter weather. *J. Wildl. Manage.* 36:892-896.

Ozoga, J. J., and E. M. Harger. 1966. Winter activities and feeding habits of northern Michigan coyotes. *J. Wildl. Manage.* 30:809-818.

Ozoga, J. J., and L. J. Verme. 1970. Winter feeding patterns of penned white-tailed deer. *J. Wildl. Manage.* 34:431-439.

Ozoga, J. J., and L. J. Verme. 1982. Physical and reproductive characteristics of a supplementally-fed white-tailed deer herd. *J. Wildl. Manage.* 46:281-301.

Parker, G. R., and J. W. Maxwell. 1989. Seasonal movements and winter ecology of the coyote, *Canis latrans,* in northern New Brunswick. *Canadian Field-Naturalist* 103:1-11.

Pielou, E. C. 1991. *After the Ice Age: the return of life to glaciated North America.* The University of Chicago Press, Chicago, Il. 366 pp.

Robinson, W. L. 1960. Test of shelter requirements of penned white-tailed deer. *J. Wildl. Manage.* 24:364-371.

Robinson, W. L. 1962. Social dominance and physical condition among penned white-tailed deer fawns. *J. Mammal.* 43:462-469.

Rongstad, O. J., and J. R. Tester. 1969. Movements and habitat use of white-tailed deer. *J. Wildl. Manage.* 33:366-379.

Schorger, A. W. 1953. *The white-tailed deer in early Wisconsin.* Wisconsin Acad. Sci., Arts and Letters 42:197-245.

Severinghaus, C. W. 1982. Sex and age composition of winter -killed deer in the central Adirondack region of New York. *New York Fish and Game J.* 29:199-203.

Shiras, G. III. 1921. The wildlife of Lake Superior, past and present. *Nat. Geographic.* 40:113-204.

Silver, H., N. F. Colovos, J. B. Holter, and H. H. Haynes. 1969. Fasting metabolism of white-tailed deer. *J. Wildl. Manage.* 33:490-498.

Sparrowe, R. D., and P. F. Springer. 1970. Seasonal activity patterns of white-tailed deer in eastern South Dakota. *J. Wildl. Manage.* 34:420-431.

Tierson, W. C., G. F. Mattfeld, R. W. Sage, Jr. and D. F. Behrend. 1985. Seasonal movements and home ranges of white -tailed deer in the Adirondacks. *J. Wildl. Manage.* 49:760 -769.

Ullrey, D. E., W. G. Youatt, H. E. Johnson, P. K. Ku, and L. D. Fay. 1964. Digestibility of cedar and aspen browse for the white-tailed deer. *J. Wildl. Manage.* 28:791-797.

Ullrey, D. E., W. G. Youatt, H. E. Johnson, L. D. Fay, and B. L. Bradley. 1967. Protein requirement of white-tailed deer fawns. *J. Wildl. Manage.* 31:679-685.

Ullrey, D. E., H. E. Johnson, W. G. Youatt, L. D. Fay, B. L. Schoepke, and W. T. Magee. 1971. A basal diet for deer nutrition research. *J. Wildl. Manage.* 35:57-62.

Ullrey, D. E., W. G. Youatt, H. E. Johnson, L. D. Fay, R. L. Covert, and W. T. Magee. 1975. Consumption of artificial browse supplements by penned white-tailed deer. *J. Wildl. Manage.* 39:699-704.

Verme, L. J. 1965. Swamp conifer deeryards in northern Michigan: Their ecology and management. *J. Forestry* 63:523-529.

Verme, L. J. 1968. An index to winter weather severity for northern deer. *J. Wildl. Manage.* 32:566-574.

Verme, L. J. 1973. Movements of white-tailed deer in upper Michigan. *J. Wildl. Manage.* 37:545-552.

Verme, L. J. 1977. Assessment of natal mortality in upper Michigan deer. *J. Wildl. Manage.* 41:700-708.

Verme, L. J., and J. J. Ozoga. 1971. Influence of winter weather on white-tailed deer in Upper Michigan. Pages 16-28 in A. O. Haugen, ed. *Proc. Snow and Ice Symposium,* Iowa State Univ.

Verme, L. J., and J. J. Ozoga. 1980. Influence of protein-energy intake on deer fawns in autumn. *J. Wildl. Manage.* 44:305-314.

Verme, L. J., and J. J. Ozoga. 1980. Effects of diet on growth and lipogenesis in deer fawns. *J. Wildl. Manage.* 44:315-324.